GUARDING THE FLAME

Guarding the Flame

The Challenges Facing the Church in the Twenty-First Century

A Conversation With Cardinal Peter Erdő

Robert Moynihan
and
Viktoria Somogyi

*Translated into English from the original
Italian by Christopher Hart-Moynihan*

TAN Books
Charlotte, North Carolina

To all who have kept the faith

CONTENTS

A NOTE TO READERS

THIS BOOK was prepared on the basis of four days of interviews with Cardinal Erdő in his residence in Budapest in the summer of 2011 and three days of interviews in New York City in January of 2018.

PREFACE

In a lecture delivered on January 29, 2018, at Columbia University, a Hungarian cardinal, in a magisterial address, argued that free societies must draw on the wisdom of religious faith to confront the moral and social problems facing the modern world.

Cardinal Peter Erdő, Archbishop of Esztergom-Budapest, delivered the Bampton Lecture at Columbia University on Monday, January 29, 2018. The Bampton Lectures in America were created in 1948 and feature talks from theologians, scientists, and artists.

Addressing Columbia students and faculty, Erdő warned against the dangers of moral relativism and suggested that the Church has an essential role even in a secular state.

The cardinal said that relativism—the unwillingness to declare anything objectively "right" or "wrong," "good or "evil"—is a "grave crisis" for all the modern secular states. Without a foundation in natural law, he argued, societies become unstable and moral evil becomes permissible and may flourish.

Erdő was chosen to deliver the lecture in 2018 because he is eminent for his intelligence, wisdom, and culture. He brought to his talk a lifetime of experience as a researcher in the history and theory of law, both civil and canon, and as a leader of the Church in Hungary and in Europe—as twice president for five years of the Council of European

Bishops' Conference (CCEE), and as one of the heads, on the Catholic side, of a decade-long dialogue between Catholics and Orthodox on social and cultural issues facing the world today, a "globalized" world dominated by a culture that tends to marginalize the very concept of "God."

Some years ago, in the summer of 2011, still during the pontificate of Benedict XVI, I visited Erdő's home in Budapest, Hungary, and spent several days with him. The interview lasted for four entire days. I had planned to publish the content right away, but the weight of other work delayed the conclusion of the project for several years. The book finally appeared in Italian, published by the Vatican Press, in the summer of 2015, and now, in 2019, for the first time, in English.

Erdő, one of the cardinals most respected by the bishops of Europe, was born in Budapest on June 25, 1952. He turned sixty-six in the summer of 2018. He studied theology at the Archbishop's Seminary in Esztergom and at the major seminary of the capital, Budapest, then was ordained on June 18, 1975, when he was still twenty-three.

On November 5, 1999, he was appointed auxiliary bishop of Székesfehérvár. He received his episcopal consecration from Pope John Paul II on January 6, 2000, in Saint Peter's Basilica in the Vatican. With the resignation of Cardinal Laszlo Paskai upon reaching the age limit, on December 7, 2002, Erdő was appointed archbishop of Esztergom-Budapest and, at the same time, Primate of Hungary.

In the consistory of October 21, 2003, he was created and proclaimed cardinal and received the titular church of Santa Balbina. Until November 20, 2010, he was the youngest of all the cardinals, a distinction he then ceded to

Reinhard Marx, fifteen months younger. He was elected president of the Hungarian Catholic Bishops' Conference in 2005. From 2006 until 2016, for two five-year terms, he also served as the president of the Council of European Bishops' Conferences.

INTRODUCTION TO THE FIRST ITALIAN EDITION

ON A lovely, sunny day in Budapest, Hungary, the cardinal celebrated morning Mass in the chapel in his residence. We had a spartan breakfast of bread and rolled oat flakes along with his two assistants, Father Zoltán Kovács and Father László Monostori. We then walked down the corridor to the cardinal's study and began our discussion, which continued for four days. During the discussion, Erdő spoke of his faith, of his life, of the challenges facing the Church, of his mission as a priest and bishop, and of his vision for human dignity and freedom in a Europe that is not only "post-Communist" but also "post-Christian." And as he sketched his vision for a renewal of the Christian faith in the twenty-first century, for a "new evangelization" that can effectively reach young people and inspire them to return to the faith and practices of the Catholic Church, it became clear that Erdő is a figure who is not only building bridges between the separated Christians of the Orthodox and Catholic worlds, helping Europe to "breathe with two lungs," in the words of Pope John Paul II, but also between the older and the younger generations. This quiet, learned, holy man, respected by his fellow bishops in Europe, Africa, and around the world, could be a strong voice for the renewal of society following many decades of severe repression, first under the Communists, then under the relativists, who now dominate Western society and culture. Here are excerpts from our conversation.

PART I

LIFE

Out of the Crucible: The Life and
Vocation of a Man of Faith

CHAPTER 1

FAMILY AND CHILDHOOD

*"Unfortunately, his beautiful library was destroyed in '56
when the Soviet tanks destroyed also our own house."*

LET'S START with your family. Tell me something about
your childhood and upbringing.

Our family was a Catholic family. The faith was woven
into the fabric of our life. Each evening, my parents prayed
together and, little by little, invited us also to pray with
them. I particularly remember the season of Advent. Every
Saturday night turned into a little celebration, reading a
passage of the Bible, then singing with a candle. During
that season, my mother prepared baked apples, which did
not cost much, but they were something special, and so we
had something interesting to eat. In this way, we waited
for the baby Jesus. We also prepared the way for the baby
Jesus: we made little rugs out of paper, to make the stable
where he would be born more beautiful. She told us that
each yellow or red strip that we wove into the fabric stood
for some good deed that we had done, and so we knew
that we had to do some good things in order to bring those
strands into the weaving—pray or help in the kitchen or
do something else, maybe go willingly to the store, or help

3

mother around the house and so on. Later we made small shirts for the baby Jesus, and she told us we could draw little crosses on the shirt when we did something good. And in this way, we prepared for Christmas Day.

Also, for Easter, there were some family traditions that my parents, who were intellectuals, wanted to stay at home. They belonged to a group of large Catholic families in Budapest, something which then was totally secret, of course, led by a good priest who had previously been a professor in Vienna, Imre Mihalik, who was later, as a refugee in America, a professor at a seminary. He died some time ago. I believe he lived in New Orleans.

Your parents, what were their names?

Sándor Erdő was my father; my mother was Mária Kiss.

What memories do you have of your father?

He died at the age of sixty-one, suddenly. He had an illness that affected his heart. We immediately said that he was a very good man because God had in this way shown his love for him, not asking him to suffer very much. My father was very gentle; he had a big heart. He had a remarkable memory, and he knew how to calculate sums very well, without paper, without a computer, which didn't yet exist: very well, almost like a professional. Then he was an excellent bridge player, which also requires a certain logic. In his youth, he had even won some bridge tournaments.

He was deeply Catholic but not at all a religious conservative. He was someone who loved French Catholicism, especially that of the 1950s. He knew the best authors of the period before the Second World War. He attended the high school of the Budapest Benedictines, then studied law, but he could never work as a lawyer because he was too Catholic. He never became involved in politics, and if he could have chosen, maybe he would have been a Catholic more of the left than of the right. But life never offered him the possibility of working in the field of the law because the simple fact that he went to church discredited him. So he worked first as a laborer, then as an assistant of accounting at various firms, and so went his life.

But at home, he told us many things. Unfortunately, his beautiful library, which he had gathered, burned in 1956 when the Soviet tanks destroyed our house. So we were for a certain time homeless; then, in a workers' hospice, we found a room and there we spent the most difficult weeks, eating very delicious things, previously unknown to us, that arrived in cardboard boxes with the words "Gift of the American people" written on the outside. After the defeat of the revolution of '56, these parcels came, and we ate from those parcels for many months. And then we also received clothes because everything we owned was burned. Only the clothes we had had on our backs when we fled were left.

And slowly, bit by bit, life returned to normal in about a year, because even after the revolution, it was a troubled period, then the streets of Budapest were repaired, with the help of the Soviet Union—it was probably too negative as propaganda to leave the city center completely destroyed. In the last months, we were separated. At the time, there were three of us, three brothers—my sisters were born later. We were divided among three peasant families, in a village near Budapest, which was something organized by the Catholic Church. A parish priest found the families for us. At that time, farmers still owned their lands. The Communists had not yet managed to introduce the Kolkhoz, or collective farm-system, which was introduced in the early '60s. Thus the peasants had food to eat that the city people did not have. So these families could accommodate an additional child, but not three, and we were placed in three different families, and so we were able to survive for another three or four months.

After that, we were able to return to Budapest and to be together again with our parents.

But religion and faith, belonging to the Church, always played a role in our lives. I've spoken about some of my earliest memories. Then I attended a church, the parish church where I was also baptized, in Józsefváros (a Budapest district), which also had a very intense parish life. There were groups of altar boys. The assistant parish priest prepared us to serve Mass. Every week there was a meeting, which was quite interesting, with a bit of catechesis.

In school, during the first two years, there was still at that time a weekly religion class, but the priests who taught the class were arrested, one after another, and in the end, there was no longer any religious instruction.

There was religious education in some distant parishes, though not in the schools, and that's when my father said, "This is unacceptable, I will have to teach you myself." And so he did, every Sunday: in the morning, we went to Mass, then after Mass, before lunch, he taught us catechism.

There were books, small catechisms, the only ones that could be printed legally in the country.

Because?

Because the author was the president at the time of the bishops' conference, Msgr. Endre Hamvas, of whom later it was said that perhaps he was too complacent with the Communist regime, though no trace of anything compromising has ever been discovered against him. Indeed, before the war, he was very esteemed as a catechist, and also for his scholarly research. He focused on catechesis and was vicar general of Cardinal Serédi, the predecessor of Cardinal Mindszenty. And this old bishop was the only one who could risk publishing a catechism. I can show the book to you. They were very simple, but the substance was there.

And so my father taught us, using these catechisms, for many years. So when I started high school with my twin brother at the Piarists' school, which was the only Catholic school still open in the city, there was an initial examination, where they tried to see the extent of our knowledge about religion. And we were among the best, meaning that my father had taught us well. And I say this because he taught us not only what was in these simple catechisms but also gave us many compulsory readings.

For example, in the sixth and seventh grade, we had to read the entire New Testament, and in the eighth grade, the *Jewish War* of Flavius Josephus, *De bello Judaico*, and this made a very deep impression on me, to read this also together in the family. My father was oriented in this way, and with great responsibility, he offered us also these texts to read and learn from.

So, I think it was good preparation. And we not only heard, but we saw that our parents paid personally for their faith. My mother was a teacher but could not teach because she was too Catholic.

Then, of course, there was always the economic scarcity in the family. Certainly, a good judge or lawyer earns more, right?

Do you have a specific memory of your father?

Of course. He had a calm mind, serene. He knew how to enjoy life. He made for us, for example, some color-coded cards on the history of art, of literature, philosophy, various European nations, and playing with these cards we could learn the names of the "greats," and learn about Leonardo da Vinci, Lev Tolstoj, or Bramante. And this was also a beautiful thing that he did with pleasure.

A moment of sadness?

There were moments of sadness, partly due to our economic conditions, partly due to the uncertainty of his work, although under socialism, inevitably at least one in the family was required to have a job. But to work in a bad place or a distant place, this could be a cause of sadness. Or when we heard that he had been humiliated at his workplace. There is a moment that I must tell you about, and after I will explain.

My father was, in the mid-seventies, section chief in his

office, working for a company in the construction sector. They were building roads. And once he came home saying, "Ah, I'm no longer the section chief, I'm just an advisor now."

"What happened? They weren't happy with your work?"

"No, actually, I'm doing the work of three men."

"So, what happened?"

"I went to the editor and asked him why. And he said: 'What do you think? Your son was ordained a priest last week. You can't be section chief any longer.'"

I was that son. This was a moment of sadness or joy, or, I don't know, perhaps a mixture of the two.

So, thank you for those memories. And your mother? Do you remember anything about your mother?

My mother was a very dynamic person, who could organize the affairs not only of a family but of the entire community.

My mother, in her youth, in the '40s, was a leader of the Marian Congregation, and she organized small groups who went out to villages that had been practically abandoned to take care of children, girls, and people in those areas who had been very neglected. She also had many intellectual pursuits, learned about government, *et cetera*, and when she became a teacher, it was evident that she had a special gift for art. She knew how to draw very well. There were others among her relatives, in her extended family, who were artists. There was also a sculptor. And then my mother wanted to study art, but even at the academy of art there was an entrance examination, and there they said, "If you enter the Communist youth organization, and accept a high posting,

at the national level, as you had in the Marian Congregation, you will be admitted."

And she immediately said, "No thank you, I cannot."
And they responded, "Why not? Your social background
meets our criteria." And her father was now retired, but
he was still a railway employee and drove these suburban
trains which linked the suburbs with the city center, and
because of this, they said, "Okay. She isn't a class enemy."
However, she was too religious, so she could not be admitted. And, then, later, during the era of political transition,
in '89, when my father had already died, my mom immediately joined the Smallholders Party, which was the party
that had won the first elections after the Second World
War. She remembered that and thought she could do
something again for the public good, for the people. Then
naturally she was disappointed because the revival was not
like her memories from a few decades before.

Is she still alive?

No, she died in '92.

Do you have a brother?

I have two brothers. A twin brother (died in 2014), a
younger brother, and three sisters.

So you are the oldest?

Yes.

And older than your brother by how many minutes?

Ten minutes.

And that was important?

Maybe yes, because I was a bit bigger. Then it was important because the tradition in the family was that the eldest son was always Sándor (Alexander) for many generations; even my dad was Sándor. But because we were twins and we were born near the feast of Saints Peter and Paul, we became Peter and Paul. And then the third son was Sándor.

And what is the first memory you have? Your first memories of life . . .

They are just images.

At what age?

About two, three years old. Surely at four and a half years old, what happened in '56, as far as I could understand it as a child, this is present. I remember completely because things were so unusual. It's not every day that one's family's home is destroyed.

Were you near the house at the time?

I was at home.

At home? Just in the house?

And then we had to take refuge in another place, then in the basement, then when there was a bit of silence we left the house.

But you remember that day?

Yes, of course. Not the date, but all of the events.

What do you remember?

We were eating at the table. It was breakfast, and a bullet went through the room above. So my grandfather—because at that time we were together with my grandparents— immediately said, "We should leave the room." We left the room, and we went back into the kitchen, which was furthest from the window. Then the shooting continued, and finally, a shot shook the house, and then we ran out of the apartment because what was happening was so much worse than what we had expected. My grandparents were used to it because during the war the whole town had been living in cellars—the cellars were large because, first of all, people wanted a lot of space for wood and coal, in order to have heat through the winter, and then also for safety. Some houses had been built using this type of thinking. Our house was one of the houses of the late nineteenth century.

But it was an apartment?

Where we lived was just an apartment. But the house was big. A house with five floors. Made of brick, one of these traditional houses. Not out of wood like in America, eh!

Do you remember anything from your life in the Church, such as baptism?

Not baptism, because of course I was baptized at three days old. Then it was still one of the first things to be done when one was born, no? The baptism.

But was it not already a political act to be baptized?

No, not so much. To have one's children baptized was inconvenient for party officials, army officers, police. But for ordinary people this was not a great sin, to baptize their children. Giving them special education, or if they attended religious instruction, this was already another matter . . .

Then . . . the language. You learned the Hungarian language.

Yes.

How did this language seem to you?

Well, I really had no way to compare it with any other because at home my parents spoke Hungarian. It was some years later when I began to understand that my grandparents sometimes spoke some other language. It was always before Christmas when they were talking about presents. We wrote a letter when we were six or seven years old to the baby Jesus, writing down what we wanted as a present. And as we wrote, there was a discussion between our parents and grandparents that we did not understand. And that was in

German. Then we realized later that when it came to gifts for our parents, our grandparents used another language, a very secret language, which was Romanian, because they had come from present-day Romania, my paternal grand-parents, and so they knew three languages. Certainly, we spoke Hungarian at home, but we knew a bit of the others as well.

And there was the liturgy in the church . . .

It was beautiful, mystical, but also the priests celebrated Mass with respect, and some of them also had a reputation for being very brave, very holy, or even in danger of being arrested, so my parents would whisper, "This priest is a very good person, pray for him because maybe he will be taken away." Things like that.

Were you an altar boy?

Yes, of course.

Do you have any memories of pronouncing the words in Latin?

Sure. I still know them. *Introibo ad altare Dei. Ad Deum qui laetificat iuventutem meam. Iudica me, Deus, et discerne causam meam de gente non sancta: ab homine iniquo et doloso erue me. Quia tu es, Deus, fortitudo mea: quare me repulisti, et quare tristis incedo, dum affligit me inimicus?* (I will go up to the altar of God. To God who gives joy to my youth. Judge me, O God, and distinguish my cause from the nation that is not holy: deliver me from the unjust and deceitful man. Because you are my strength, why hast thou rejected me and why am I downcast, while the enemy afflicts me?)

Do you have any memories of mystical moments or moments in which you questioned human existence or the existence of God?

At that age, no. Later. In that age, I think we had a faith that grew naturally. At the age of six, we went to the first Communion with great devotion, and immediately after, we received Confirmation because it was rumored that perhaps the last bishops would be arrested. So everyone now was asking to be confirmed, because later there would perhaps be no more bishops able to do it. People knew that the pope may also appoint a priest to administer the sacrament of Confirmation. However, the general feeling was that the real Confirmation is administered by the bishop.

At that time, the diocese was governed by Msgr. Endrei. Sometime after '56, a former auxiliary bishop of another diocese governed our diocese *ad interim*, as a delegate. But they made him depart shortly thereafter, and then came Msgr. Artur Schwartz-Eggenhofer, who was first appointed as vicar-capitular, then apostolic administrator. He was a canon of Esztergom, but not a bishop, so the fears were also somewhat justified.

Do you remember any moment from your confirmation? The ceremony?

Yes, of course. It was in Saint Stephen's Basilica. There were many people and for us it was a long ceremony, but beautiful, and outside the basilica were the street vendors who offered us these small prayer cards with the Heart of Jesus, perhaps as a "reminder of your Confirmation," with the date, and so on.

Did you take a name?

Yes, Ladislaus.

Ladislaus. Why?

Because my godfather took the name Ladislaus at his confirmation; he was a friend of my father. There was no great theological choice. It was a traditional thing, of course.

Were there any saints whom you studied in those years who were your favorites?

At such a young age I listened a little to the stories of my parents, and there even was a big book in our home with the lives of the saints with pictures, very well done. Today I would say that the authors were learned men, serious scholars.

Do you remember the book?

Yes, because it was a very popular book, a large volume. Sure.

Do you remember the professor?

Polykárp Radó, who published, for example, two large volumes, *Enchiridion liturgicum*, at Herder in Rome, just at the dawn of the Second Vatican Council—so a bit too late, but he was a very profound scholar, Benedictine, whom my father knew well. His book in Hungarian about the saints was in our home and my parents, sometimes, would read the life of some saint.

Do you remember any saints in particular?

Yes . . . Saints Peter and Paul.

What was striking in Peter and Paul?

The princes of the apostles, it called them, the two leaders, the most important ones. The two pillars of the Church of Rome. Then their martyrdom; then later in the book, what Saint Clement of Rome wrote in his letter to the Corinthians. Saint Clement writes that it was the contrast, the conflict between brothers, which had caused the death of the princes of the apostles. And therefore, he admonished the faithful in Corinth to be united.

Saint Peter, of course, as my patron saint. He was a man who did not think about himself a great deal; that is, he was humble. However, he had certainty in the substantive things. And he took on a very special mission that was received from Jesus. He had a special clarity that grew out of his special love for Jesus Christ, and above all out of

God's grace, out of the free choice of the Lord. Then, Saint Philip Neri, and Saint Francis de Sales.

Why Saint Francis de Sales?

The patron saint of bishops! I have read his works several times . . . his life, I visited Thonon, I visited the sites of his life.

But what was his most profound advice for pastors?

His gentleness, his prudence in speaking with people who thought differently. His strength in arguing in a patient way, in a respectful manner. And his love for the Church and the Catholic faith.

Then later, when I was already thirteen years old, I started, following the advice of my confessor, to read more serious books, immediately throwing myself into the sea, Saint Teresa of Avila, then the *Philothea* of Saint Francis de Sales, the *Theotimus* of Francis de Sales, also certainly *Imitatio Christi*, attributed to Thomas a Kempis, these things.

And this at thirteen, fourteen . . . What impact did it have?

A great impact. That was the moment when I thought for the first time that perhaps I had to become a priest.

CHAPTER 2

VOCATION

"The reality of God began to attract me."

WHY DID you want to become a priest?

Because the reality of God began to attract me, in the liturgy as an altar boy, in reading, in prayer.

What was the reality of God, more concretely?

The reality which explained many things in life to me. It explained the world, explained to me my place in the world, and also explained what I had to do in life.

Almost like a *logos*, a *telos*.

Yes, something that comprehends all and that gives light, gives meaning, to all things.

What was it that you had to do in life? What was this vocation?

The clearest voice, and the most fundamental, told me to seek the will of God and carry it out. Then, something else might come into my mind: "Careful, you still haven't prepared your homework for tomorrow, you should do it now and then take a walk after." That was how I did things.

Was that voice your conscience, or . . . your father?

Not my father. My conscience. Or really, the Bible. My confessor also recommended for me to read a page, a small page, of the New Testament every day, and meditate on it for five minutes. Not even for fifteen minutes; for five minutes. And the end of the meditation always brought some good idea or suggestion. So, if today I still haven't done anything to bring joy, to bring a little happiness, to my mom, to my brothers, so what can I do? Every day, just a little thing. And this was very good, especially when I was able to do it. After I did one thing, the next time it was much easier.

And the beginning is everything. Every long voyage begins with a single step.

Yes, this was one experience. Then I began to go to church and take Communion or pray every day, even when I had to read. The personal encounter with Jesus meant a lot to me. And after Communion, I would remain in prayer for a few minutes.

To find the will of God, and follow it?

Yes, and also to talk to Christ, as to a friend.

We are speaking of "vocation." How can you tell? Does one hear a voice? Where do you hear this?

Of course in the mind, or in the heart. Not physically. Perhaps in certain situations. Some situations have, or may have, either a symbolic meaning or a realistic meaning which has a deeper meaning at the same time. In life, there are situations that occur on different planes of reality. Much later, for example, I read Bulgakov, *The Master and Margarita*.

Do you remember such a situation from those years?

That had this deeper meaning? I was already in high school. Once I had a dream. In the dream, I saw that I was physically standing in front of a coffin and I knew—I cannot explain how—that it was one of my teachers, a Piarist, who was our math teacher. He had been perhaps a bit sick at that time, but we didn't know that it was anything serious. I was standing there, behind me was the coffin, and in front of me a crowd of young people, and priests, and I was speaking to them about this professor. This was the dream I had while the professor was still alive. Later, he had to go to the hospital and a few months later he died.

Then our head teacher, the professor who guided us as an educator—I do not know, perhaps in America there is also this figure—who was a relatively old Piarist father, a very good specialist in grammar and style, said, "We must choose someone to make the speech for the deceased, on behalf of the students." And they chose me. Then we went to the cemetery, where the coffin was sitting to my back, just like in the dream, and I had to speak to the people, as in the dream. The dream came true.

I did not know then and I don't know even now what kind of experience this was, perhaps an experience of dimensions of human reality that we still know little about. I would not go so far as to say that it was a case of a super-natural experience, because we know still so little about nature, and yet it was an experience "above" nature. Any-way, for me, it was an interesting situation.

Another situation, much more personal, is a religious experience, when one sees some big problem, maybe a brother in trouble, or with an illness or some other prob-lem. And it seems as though nothing good can happen, and in that moment, you make a promise to God that you will do this and that if . . . and the next day the problem is resolved.

Did this happen?

Yes, of course, these are the small miracles that strongly convince the person who experiences them, although for others they may sound less convincing.

Yes, they are the ways of the Lord. From one point of view, everything may seem random, but from another point of view, they are miracles.

They have a personal aspect, they take place in a context of personal dialogue with Christ. In that context, they have a deeper meaning.

Can it be said that in some ways you have seen miracles?

In this sense, yes.

And how have you experienced the divine presence in the liturgy, both then and later, after the liturgical reform in the '60s?

In Hungary, this change was not such a big thing. As Cardinal Dziwisz has said about Poland, I have also had this same experience. When, after the Council, these instructions began to arrive, then the clergy responded as it could, not that we had any possibility to print books, et cetera. Nor were there many specialists to make good translations.

Our Church reacted with a certain slowness since we were faced with much more concrete and serious problems. Neither the clergy nor the people felt a great need for a liturgical reform because we were happy just to still have open churches. But everyone, almost everyone, accepted it. Everyone thought, "Okay, if the Holy See sees it this way, we will certainly do it like that." However, given the external difficulties, everything was not done so radically, but it was more gradual, more organic, so few had a negative impression of the reform. There were perhaps some exaggerations, but nothing too radical, and they were not general.

Your education continued, but in which school? Was it a Benedictine school?

No. Piarist. In Budapest at that time, for boys, there were only the Piarists.

And were there boys and also girls, or just . . . ?

For girls, there was another school. Back in that time, there were separate schools for boys and girls even in the state education.

Did you always go to school only with boys? All of your school years?

Yes, but never to boarding school. We lived at home. The school was nearby.

Then came the end of high school. And then? University?

In the last year of high school, you had to fill out the official form that they had prepared, which was a government form, and with this form, you could request admission to any college or university. It was a complicated system because in the framework of the planned economy the number of available places for any field of study was also planned. There were plans that anticipated how many engineers of one or another type would be needed, how many professors of one language or another, and so they had determined the number already from the beginning.

Then there were the entrance exams, which were very difficult, so theoretically only the best were admitted. Then there were some political, and also official, criteria, such as, for example, the percentage of students according to their social background. A certain percentage had to come from working-class families, a certain percentage from peasant families, a certain percentage from intellectuals. This was a rule of law. It was not something hidden or secret. Then there was a legal provision which gave a privilege to holders of some state honor, maybe the honor of the socialist fatherland, who were fighters against the revolution of '56, and their children or grandchildren had precedence when it came to university admissions. This too was a rule of law sanctioned in the official bulletin.

Then there was something else too, which was not in the official bulletin, but was in a circular newsletter received by the universities, which said that the few students who had taken a graduation examination in a high school of the Church could not be recruited to certain departments, for example to the humanities, law, and so on. But up to a certain percentage we could be accepted to the departments of natural sciences. Among my high school classmates are experts in nuclear physics, astronomy, many who now work in the computing world, some even have become quite rich, but there is no professor of history, no one who studied philosophy, and so on. There is one who became a lawyer, but how? After the graduation exam, he went to work as a laborer in a print shop and joined the party and later he was admitted to the university and was able to study law.

But was he really a Communist?

No, not at all. He just wanted to have his papers in order. As he said: one can be a Christian gentleman, but no need to be so fastidious. He considered himself a Christian gentleman, but he didn't want to be too, let us say, sensitive. There was also this attitude.

At that time, how did you perceive the struggle between Church and State, between Christianity and Communism, the struggle between the old and the new Hungary?

We did not feel involved in a fight, and we didn't feel at all that the Church represented a Hungary older than the present one because we had information, despite everything, about the world Church and we had the impression that, even with regard to intellectual currents, the Church was advanced. It didn't seem at all like a backward segment of society, nor did our school, which was, after all, very good.

We had, rather, the sense of being under an enormous weight. Not as participants in a struggle, but subjects under an enormous weight. Because if one is brave, one can sustain a struggle with an enemy five times stronger, but when an enemy is two hundred times stronger, then it is not about fighting anymore. And above all, the Hungarians in their history have always had the experience of being abandoned and betrayed by the West, which they had wanted to defend, and to which they felt they belonged. So even in the time of the Turks and also later, this was repeated many times, as it was in '56, and so forth. So this feeling was also present.

Did you have to perform military service and learn to use weapons?

Yes, I had to do a year of military service. During this year, I noticed that some students of theology who were together with us carried rosaries. This was a bit risky because it was forbidden, and if they had found one, perhaps they would have punished the soldier, and then they would have trampled the rosary. So I thought, "I have ten fingers, I don't need to carry a rosary with me and take the risk." But then I discovered another rosary during the long hours of the night watch when we would stand guard with a Kalashnikov. The Kalashnikov had ten holes, and over these ten holes in the side of the Kalashnikov, I could quietly pray the rosary, and it was very nice. I never would skip even one *Ave Maria*.

CHAPTER 3

PRIESTHOOD

"Helping people in the most important thing, in the matter
of salvation, seemed, and still seems to me, something
so important as to deserve dedicating one's life to it."

MAY I ask a delicate question? If you do not want to
respond, you do not have to. Choosing the way of the
priesthood, there was the decision not to seek the path of
marriage and of creating a family. Was it a difficult choice?

In order to fill out that official form in the last year of high
school, where one had to indicate where one wished to
study, we had to study again after the exams, and that was
the moment. Not like today, where everybody can decide at
any time where to study, but you had to fill out this form.
Once it was filled out, it was decided. For example, putting
the Esztergom seminary meant that I could not present
myself at the entrance examinations of any other universities, and although I was not obliged before the state to go
to the seminary, practically, there was no longer any question [that I would go].

But before filling out the form, it was a vocational
decision. Already when I was thirteen, the thought was
beginning to come once in a while, but not the decision.

The decision was not like today, without an endpoint, without a time limit. There was a limit. You were supposed to decide by this deadline. And I prayed a lot before completing the form. A priest took me to the Esztergom seminary, which was not the building we have now, but just the provisional headquarters we occupied for forty years. Then at the seminary, I was able to see how the candidates lived, how everything was structured, and I didn't get scared, so I presented myself there and I was convinced that this was the will of God.

And what was it, love for the Church and for God, that led you to give your life to this service?

Most certainly, the importance of the priestly ministry for the salvation of souls, the world, the administration of the sacraments, even the announcement of the Word of God with special strength in the power of the sacrament, which is a qualitative difference. Helping people in the most important thing, in the matter of salvation, seemed, and still seems to me, something so important as to deserve dedicating one's life to it. I also thought, just as a dream, that it would be nice to become a doctor in order to help the sick. But then it seemed much more important to me to be a priest. And then, I did not have much of a technical interest, as some of my fellow seminarians did. One was also an engineer because he wanted to serve society with his work, but then he found that there are still more important issues. The importance of ministering to address them was the decisive thing.

Then, after years of preparation, you were ordained a priest at the age of twenty-three. What were your emotions at the moment of your ordination?

The great joy of being able to serve as a priest and the great joy of a new personal relationship with Jesus Christ.

What happened on that day?

That day I was ordained not in the cathedral but in the parish church because Cardinal Lékai, who was then still not a cardinal, said that it was necessary to ordain a priest every year in Budapest so that the people could see that this thing still exists. And so I was ordained in Budapest. And after the ordination and the Mass, there was a dinner at the parish.

Which year? Which day?

That was in 1975. On June 22.

Were there other priests?

No, it was only me because the others were ordained in the cathedral here in Esztergom. There were not many of us. We started with fifteen, and only three or four were ordained.

But the ones who left . . . these were in the years 1972, 1973?

Between 1970 and 1975.

But were there some infiltrators? Were there government spies?

Yes, always. But it was a bit difficult to say who were true infiltrators among us or among our professors, or who were simply weak—young men who went home and talked too much and then one of their relatives had some contacts with the regime. But we all knew that the authorities were well informed about what went on in the seminary. We were in the crosshairs.

But was it an atmosphere of fear or . . . ?

No. We did not take the situation so tragically. There was serenity, there was a very good humor among us. I don't know if you are familiar with the novel of Imre Kertész, which was awarded the Nobel Prize. It's a novel of his experiences in Auschwitz, in the death camps, as a young man who was deported. The book came out also in English; the title is *Fatelessness*. Kertész writes that in the camps, everything seemed natural although the situation was anything but natural and normal. Because although it was not normal, they, in their daily course of events, had the feeling or sense of a certain banality or normality. And so, similarly, we too felt it natural that the authorities were certainly observing everything, that they would know everything, but nevertheless, we did not feel bad in the seminary.

But did people think that Communism would last for centuries, for decades?

Yes, of course. It was a surprise when they said in '88 that perhaps Communism would end because in Hungary, given the presence of Soviet troops, there was no possibility of change. As long as Soviet troops were there, both the intellectuals and the common people had all adapted themselves to this situation.

And did you think that the Church would continue to exist?

Of course, no one thought that the Church could be exterminated. No, no. Of course, the statistics were already discouraging. In '85 the statistics were the same as today in terms of both the number of vocations and Church attendance. Today we have almost the same pastoral result, but with far greater commitment at the institutional level because we also have schools, we have many facilities, many expenses, but the bottom line remains the same. Yet, we must undertake all these other activities, these efforts, because, in this context of greater freedom, the competition is much greater.

But was there never a moment in which the Communist ideals seemed attractive?

For us, never! I never had this temptation. And I also never had in my life the temptation to believe the official books, or the radio, or TV. Never, never. Perhaps because of my education.

And that day of the ordination who was the bishop? Lékai?

Lékai was the apostolic administrator. A year later he was named archbishop and cardinal.

And your first Mass?

I celebrated my first Mass in a chapel in Budapest. I would have been gladly welcomed in any other church, but I wanted it to be that way.

And then your first pastoral duty?

I was assistant pastor in Dorog, a small town where the miners lived. There were coal mines. Now they are closed because they say it is not economically worthwhile. No one really believes that. For some reason, some choice made on the international level, they closed the mines. Who knows whether it was reasonable or not.

And the pastor was good?

He was an elderly man, a Catholic believer, a country boy, who valued culture in an almost archaic way; that is, he subscribed to a magazine, the only Catholic magazine in Hungarian. He also subscribed to an international literary magazine that existed in Hungary and he would read these two magazines from beginning to end. He prepared his sermons always writing everything by hand. He was a profoundly conservative man, living, as it were, "in the past." But we had a good relationship, normal; we never quarreled.

And was it a joy to be a pastor? Or did it cause you suffering?

I was chaplain, assistant pastor. It was a pleasure. There was a group of young people, children, old people, there was a Bible meeting every week, so I think I was able to work. I also had to substitute for some neighboring parishes. One pastor was seriously ill, the other had six months of vacation—I do not know why—and I had to replace him. I was not bored. Meanwhile, in 1976, I also defended my doctoral thesis at the Faculty of Theology in Budapest.

Celebrating baptisms, first communions and this type of thing, what emotion did you feel?

With pleasure, with joy, I would say.

Then came a change of life . . .

Already as an assistant pastor, I was working as Defender of the Bond at the diocesan tribunal of Esztergom, writing my opinions. Then, they sent me to study in Rome: canon law at the Lateran. In the beginning, it seemed that it would be for two years, then I was given a third year in which I did my doctorate. I asked for permission to do the doctorate in only one year. I defended the thesis, then I returned home.

Did you learn Italian very well?

I do not know if I learned it very well, but it was enough for my studies.

You lived at the Hungarian Pontifical Ecclesiastical Institute in Rome?

Yes, on Via Giulia #1.

In the center of Rome . . .

I was able to take many walks. I wanted also to get to know the city, the Roman memories, the Church of Rome, the cultural and ecclesiastical life of the city, because even the cultural life was new to me. I read the books of Henri Marrou and the great modern philosophers and all the literature that was not yet translated into Hungarian. So, I was immersed in a much wider horizon despite the political turmoil in Italy at that time.

Then after Rome, you returned to Hungary to teach.

Yes, I returned to Hungary, and my bishop sent me to Esztergom to teach in the seminary. I taught canon law, Church history, and for some years also moral theology.

How were those years?

Peaceful, peaceful. Constructive. In those years, the *Code of Canon Law* was released, I had the opportunity to translate it into Hungarian, and we made a very nice bilingual edition, with annotations. Then I began to prepare an instructional book, I wrote several articles, I started my professional activity.

But did you think at that time that you could become primate?

No. Not at all.

CHAPTER 4

STUDIES IN ROME

"At that time, there was a tension in the
Church, which was also felt in Rome."

So, ROME. When did you visit Rome for the first time?

The first visit was not a visit, because it was in October of 1977 to begin my studies at the Lateran.

How did you feel at that moment, coming to Rome?

First of all, emotional because being able to study in Rome meant a great opportunity, and in addition, it was the first time that I was able to spend a rather long time in a Western country. Once before, I had been in Austria for a language course for three weeks, and once, I had been in France and Belgium for a sightseeing trip of fifteen days. But overall, life in the West was quite unknown to me. On the one hand, I found myself at the Lateran University in an intellectually attractive environment, on the other hand in Italy, which was bubbling over, where there were demonstrations, strikes, riots, the assassination of Aldo Moro, and all these stories. So I saw tear gas in the streets.

Then I read several newspapers, right and left, I spoke with people, with my fellow students, which was interesting.

The university was very international. I was able to get to know on a normal, human level people of different nationalities, different cultures, from Asia, America, Africa. One of my former fellow students was martyred in Rwanda.

He was African?

Yes, he was African, a priest, then after going home he became chancellor of a diocese, and during the massacres, the entire diocesan office was massacred at once, all employees and himself. He was a very dynamic man.

It was also interesting to study the world of legal culture, historical legal culture. I had excellent professors, senior professors, among the best, like Pio Ciprotti. I even had the pleasure to hear the lectures of Olis Robleda from time to time. He was a Jesuit professor at the Gregorian University. And I had as a professor of Roman law Gabrio Lombardi. Then I had many other lay professors because at the Lateran there were many classes on civil law, general legal culture, but among the canon law specialists there were some very good Spaniards, like Anastasio Gutierrez for constitutional law and Church law with regard to religious orders, then other Claretian fathers like Javier Ochoa, who also published the series *Leges Ecclesiae* which included all ecclesiastical legislation subsequent to the code of '17. Then I had José Castaño, who later became rector of the Angelicum. He was a Dominican and a very good, well-trained teacher. So his points were very clear, very convincing. Matrimonial law, the sacraments, canonical property law were his subjects. I also had professors such as the current Cardinal Vallini, the current Cardinal Bertone, and many others. It was an interesting experience. I was an enthusiastic student. I had very good grades.

What I was greatly fascinated by was the history of canon law, the opportunity to do research even in the Vatican Library, among the manuscripts. Then Cardinal Stickler allowed me to also use his personal collection, which has remained at the Salesian University, on microfilm. Then I was really able to work. I had very good professors in the auxiliary sciences, such as paleography.

In that period, we are talking about the life of the Church almost at the moment of the transition between Paul VI and John Paul II. We were almost fifteen years after the Council, and it was almost thirty-five years ago. Can you make an assessment?

At that time there was a tension in the Church, which was also felt in Rome. At the beginning of the academic year 1977–78, the opening address was delivered by Cardinal Ciappi, who was then still the theologian of the Pontifical Household. There, he said, among other things, that the Second Vatican Council, especially the initial part, had caused so much trouble in the Church. This was news to me because in Hungary we had heard in our press, even though it was loyal to the regime, only good things about the Vatican Council. I had also come out of Hungary with the belief that the Council was a good thing.

Who knows, perhaps its implementation or how it was put into practice can be debated, as we debated it at the seminary, of course. In the early 1970s when I was a seminarian, there were also discussions between priests, between seminarians on celibacy, different things: if we should study this material or that, what does it mean to go beyond Neo-Scholasticism or to not go beyond it? What are the best texts? What should we follow when we learn dogmatic theology? And so on. They were interesting questions. Or even how to correctly interpret the Bible. All of that came to us through several magazines, especially German magazines, and in Germany, this debate was quite heated, but no one thought that the Council itself had been in error.

So Ciappi?

I needed to come to Rome to hear this voice as well. But of course, we were in some ways foreign observers. We felt that in the Church a type of clarity was needed, a choice between the new phenomena to indicate what the true result was and what was something, perhaps, less clear. There were many who called for more harmony, but very few had clear ideas on how this new harmony should come about.

Then came, just in that year, in August of 1978, the death of Paul VI, and then the election of John Paul I and his death and the election of John Paul II. Were you in Rome at that time?

At the time of the pope's death, no, because it was during the holidays, however, during my first year of study, we were received twice by Paul VI. Cardinal Lékai was close to the pope and had access to him, almost easily, and introduced a few of us, who had arrived to study. It was clear that our cardinal and the Holy Father had hope, saying that the preceding decades had been difficult, but that perhaps now even in Hungary the new generation of theologians would be able to recover what earlier was not possible. Yes, there was some hope, and we saw this directly even through certain signs of "meta-communication." The extreme kindness of Paul VI to us was truly a privilege.

After his death in the summer, I spoke with a priest in Hungary, quite old, who had previously been jailed. He said, "If the Holy Spirit has courage, the new pope will be Wyszynski." The new pope was, of course, first Luciani; then after his death, the Holy Spirit showed that it actually had even more courage, because Cardinal Wojtyla was truly a big surprise for many people.

I was in the square when they declared the result because, in October, I was already there [in Rome], and we always would go to see if the smoke was black or white. Of course, it was always gray, and then because the monsignors of the Secretariat of State had turned to face the square, I realized, "Ah, finally this gray is white," and just like that people began to gather in the square. The square was overflowing. Then came Cardinal Felici and he gave the name of the new pope. And some Italians, who heard the word *Karolum, Karlum*, as Felici spoke, thought, "Ah, Confalonieri," that is, the elderly Archbishop of Milan, who was more than seventy-five years old—they sooner thought of an already-retired Italian than a foreigner. But then came the surname and they realized that it was not him.

What emotion did you feel at that moment?

I personally felt very positively, because I had heard a great deal about Cardinal Wojtyla. I had not met him personally, but certainly, this word, the courage of the Holy Spirit, was very much alive in me.

Did you think that a man from Poland, from Eastern Europe, could change the situation also in Hungary?

Perhaps [I thought] this as well, but above all the courage of the Holy Spirit. It wasn't just the usual thoughts, is he conservative, is he progressive, is he such and such, no. He was one who had known and had suffered another reality and had a very independent and sovereign vision. And when he chose the name John Paul, we knew that all the heritage of the Council and the post-conciliar period would be preserved.

And then, his papacy—twenty-six years . . .

I personally have much to thank him for.

He was elected in the context of a "cold war" between the Soviet Union and the United States. Was the new pope "impartial" or was he, one might say, "pro-American"?

In the beginning, we thought about this quite seriously because our mass media were a bit negative, so we knew that the regime did not like him. If the regime does not like him, then perhaps America does, but we had no concrete information; nor did we see any trace of American politics in his speeches or anything that he said. Above all he spoke about God, he spoke about things much deeper than the politics of the day. He spoke of man, of human dignity. For us, he was really a revelation.

Then came the assassination attempt in 1981.

At that time, I was already back home. I was teaching in the seminary at Esztergom. We were on a trip with the seminarians, with a tour bus, and we heard what had happened on the radio. Immediately we went to a church to pray for the Holy Father. Of course, at that time, there were several assassination attempts. I don't know which was the first. The first, maybe it was against the pope, then there was also something against Ronald Reagan.

Six weeks before.

That's right, and because of this, some people tried to link the two attempts. Then there were these rumors in the media of Ali Agca, the Bulgarian connection, different things. We were sure that we would never know what happened with certainty. We were not even interested in knowing the details; rather, we were just very happy to hear that the pope had overcome this crisis and could continue his ministry.

CHAPTER 5

LIFE UNDER COMMUNISM AND THE CASE OF CARDINAL MINDSZENTY

"What does it mean to be a follower of Mindszenty? I am his successor, and this is a great honor for me. I consider him a saint."

IN THE '80s, there was the so-called *Ostpolitik*.

There was already Ostpolitik in the '70s, so saying that this policy of dialogue with the Communist world was put forward only at the moment of the political detente between America and the Soviet Union gives a bit of an exaggerated impression. Because to tell the truth, just looking at, for example, the history of the martyrdom of Bishop Meszlényi, who died in '51, we see that already under Pius XII, already under Archbishop Tardini, some very practical choices were made. For example, when the faithful bishops of a diocese were arrested by the Communist regime, one after the other, and the regime was trying to force the diocesan chapter to choose the next bishop from among the members of the pro-government peace movement, what did the Church do? Rome appointed an apostolic administrator, who was tolerated by the regime, who might have also served simultaneously as a bishop of another diocese; this was Msgr. Hamvas, the author of these catechisms, which I have spoken about—who also was the bishop of Csanád.

What did this signify?

Realpolitik. They wanted to appoint someone who was more or less acceptable, even to the regime, in order to maintain the continuity of the legitimate government of the Church.

Can Realpolitik be a good word for one who is a follower of Mindszenty?

What does it mean to be a follower of Mindszenty? I am his successor, and this is a great honor for me. I consider him a saint.

Did you know him personally?

No, I never saw him, because when I was born, he was already in prison, and when I was a seminarian, he was my bishop, but he was staying in the US embassy. Then he was brought to the West, and naturally you could not meet anyone; it was not possible to meet him, of course. But we prayed for him. My parents said that he was a brave man, that it was a lie that he had claimed all the property of the Church in '56, that that was not the case, and the discourse around him did not contain any of what the propagandists of the regime were claiming about him, of course. So, we had an image of him which was based, above all, on the memory of the faithful.

So, Realpolitik. For him, Realpolitik meant to stand firm. One might even say to be intransigent. While Realpolitik under Casaroli become a sort of way to compromise.

In certain situations; now, with the research on the story of Mindszenty, which has now gone even deeper, we see that he too held some very practical opinions. For example, when he arrived in '56 at the United States Embassy, here in Budapest, immediately thereafter came the Western journalists, and they asked him, "In your opinion, who is the legitimate prime minister of Hungary? Imre Nagy or János Kádár?" And without hesitation, he immediately said Imre Nagy. This was also Realpolitik because Imre Nagy had been elected by the Communist authorities. So he at that time was not being a Legitimist; he did not say that everything was illegal. Yet he had this moral sense; he must have thought that in this Imre Nagy had behaved appropriately. So as we can see, Mindszenty was not simply a rigid theorist. We see in his memoirs that he too had moments when there were some proposals toward the end of his time served under arrest or in jail, when he seemed to be ready to accept something, not collaboration, something in order to be able to return to governing the diocese. It is not true that he was unwilling to accept anything, but he certainly was a particularly firm man, who had this characteristic already as a parish priest. Everyone knew that he was a holy man, he had strong principles.

Then the Ostpolitik of the Vatican in the years from '70 to '80. Some saw it as treason, and others as a weakness. But how are we to judge? Also from the perspective of '89 . . .

Of course, afterward, everybody is intelligent. One must understand things in terms of the moment in which they happened. Therefore I don't think it's correct to judge what they did in the '70s according to the standards of the '90s. But we did, however, see some positive effect of this so-called Ostpolitik. Where to begin?

We were able to have bishops appointed by the pope. This meant that those who were then deemed acceptable to the state were chosen from among the best; that is, from those who were also acceptable to the Church. Therefore, in their doctrine, many times even in their spiritual life and godliness, they were often people who could be respected. Cardinal Lékai, for example, had a great heart for the Church. He had a pastoral love. Those who knew him can confirm this. We have now commemorated the twenty-fifth anniversary of his death. Those who knew him personally, they respected him, they loved him. He always worked to achieve some type of freedom, some possibility of pastoral action for the Church, despite results which were often rather discouraging. Then he had faith in the Holy See; he would say, "If the Pope has said this, then we can do it." Certainly, the change in pontificates was not easy for him personally, because he was put on a track at the time of his appointment.

Which year?

It was in '76. Then, two years later, there was a change in the papacy. But this change was not so radical, and it was not without an understanding of the reality of these countries. Saint John Paul II did not want to break with the experience of his predecessor. He wanted perhaps to add other elements, enlarge different things.

What is the long tradition of Vatican diplomacy based upon?

First of all, *libertas ecclesiae*, as always. The Church must by its very nature be free because it has a mission from Jesus Christ and not just a commission from some political authority. Then, it is a mission which is directed to all men. The Church does not have foreigners. The Church is not an enemy of anyone. As in the early Middle Ages, the situation was very delicate, where there was in Europe a Romanized population with Roman culture, and with a now-established Christianity, and then came the barbarians. What did the Church do? Of course, it continued to serve the Christian community and it had the courage to go among the so-called "barbarians," as we see with Saint Gregory the Great, who said, "They are not Angles, but angels."

And the "barbarians" of our time?

The expression used in the age of St. Gregory the Great shall be implemented in the context of that given age. The Church today meets those, who are far from the faith, or do not know Christianity at all, or who have prejudices.

All this is a part of a difficult environment, but it neverthe-less attracts us because the world needs the Gospel. And that is why St. John Paul II, in his first speech, when he said "Be not afraid," who was this directed to? Not only to those of us standing in the square but also to the Commu-nist leadership. "Open wide the doors to Christ," "Do not be afraid," because Jesus Christ does not want revenge, he does not want to hurt anyone. You need not be jealous or afraid for your country.

Were there some virtues in Marxism and Communism?

If you asked if there were any "virtues" in Marxism and Communism, then I have to remind you the Catholic teaching regarding this ideology, which is atheist, therefore anti-Christian and anti-humane. I also have to remind you of all the tragedies caused by this ideology. We witnessed this also in Hungary. The situation would be different if you asked me whether the Marxists and the Communists had any virtues. For this I should answer that sin and virtue belong to the individual, to each and every human being. The intentions shall be judged only by God.

However, there are also major problems in the period after the collapse of the wall. Our years, the last twenty years, we are a bit disappointed by freedom, which certainly we want, but it is also freedom for the forces that want to dominate and exploit. So do we perhaps need a real, thorough cri-tique also of this post-Soviet period?

Of course, the human being is always the same, so the human tendencies of selfishness, thirst for power, exist in every age. Certainly, the liberal capitalist economic system was the problem at the beginning of the twentieth century. Then, in response to this problem, there arose some false answers, like Communism and Nazism, which have been proven by history to be unable to resolve the problems of man; indeed, they threaten human dignity. But after the collapse of these false attempts, we did not arrive in paradise, but rather, the original problem returned. Certainly.

Reflecting on the years of your life, can you tell us what was the happiest moment?

Well, I could say two moments. One was when I passed the graduation exam with high marks, because it was the first big test. And the other . . . ordination.

I will add a third time which was also memorable and deep, but maybe at that age one is less emotionally sensitive. The episcopal ordination made by John Paul II in Saint Peter's Basilica, which was also a profound spiritual experience.

In which year?

In 2000.

CHAPTER 6

BISHOP AND CARDINAL

"The president of the bishops' conference said, 'Peter, you have been appointed bishop, do you accept it?'"

THE EPISCOPAL consecration was in the year 2000.

I was appointed along with another Hungarian, in November, in early November 1999. I was in Rome, because I was a working as a collaborator, not a member, as an expert priest of the Synod for Europe. And at the end of the synod, when we were preparing to enter Saint Peter's Basilica, the choir was already singing *misericordias Domini in aeternum cantabo*. ["I will sing the mercies of the Lord forever"]. I was singing, and the president of the bishops' conference said, "Peter, you have been appointed bishop, do you accept it?"

Who was it?

Msgr. István Seregély. He's retired now, he was the Archbishop of Eger.

Were you walking?

Yes, we were getting ready for the Holy Mass at the conclusion of the synod. He asked taking my answer for granted as if the offer would, of course, be accepted. I did not say no.

But what did you think, or feel?

Just what the choir was singing, no? The mercy of God, which was the word being sung at that moment. We celebrated the Mass and later, upon our return to Budapest, I was called to the nunciature as is customary.

And the same message?

We finished also that oath which is connected with the profession of faith that you have to sign, you have to speak . . .

And this was January, February?

No, in November because the ordination was on January 6.

Ah, January 6, 2000.

The Epiphany.

Ah, Epiphany. And on that day what was in your spirit, in your mind, before and during the ceremony?

I do not know, everything and nothing. The mercy of God, the duties of a bishop, vocation, challenges, the Catholic university . . . because through this appointment, on the one hand, the Catholic university, of which I was the rector, came into a more direct link with the bishops' conference. Then I became at the same time auxiliary bishop to Székesfehérvár. So, I thought also about that diocese, the history of the diocese, my friends who worked there as priests, my family. At the ordination, there were many people from the university present.

The laying on of hands . . .

Very moving. I said yesterday that Paul VI had an aura of power around him, but it was very gentle. But John Paul II had this strong aura, like a fist. One felt it immediately. Not grace, because grace is not felt physically. But John Paul II had this very strong radiance. Not everybody has it, only a few exceptional ones have it.

He laid on his hands and you became a bishop.

Then, of course, there were the prayers, there were the co-consecrating bishops and the others who were present. Marcello Zago was one of the co-consecrating bishops, as secretary of the Congregation for the Evangelization of Peoples. The other was, of course, Giovanni Battista Re.

In the moment of receiving ordination, did you feel a sense of added weight?

Not so much. I will tell you what happened upon my return from the episcopal ordination. On my first day of work back in the office of the university rector, a young student came who had never had any personal conversations with me, and he basically told me about all the problems of his life. And I thought, here is the net.

What net?

The fishermen's net. The net, which I have not cast: it's true that I have to be a fisherman of souls, but not alone. Because things happen on their own, and it is necessary to work together, to be present. In the providence of God, it is Christ who acts.

Then if you could speak about everyday life, a way of life that leads to joy? What are the duties of a Cardinal Archbishop Primate, and how do you apportion and carry out your daily life in different stages?

If one consults the Code of Canon Law, the longest canons are those that speak about the duties of parish priests and the duties of bishops. So, everything is duty. If you are over-sensitive, you can't ever sleep, because you feel responsible for everything. But of course, the possibilities are limited. (Laughs)

But can you take us through a day in your life?

No, no, because greater forces always intervene if something happens in public life, or if something happens in the life of the diocese. . . . Of course, you must plan out your schedule but always with the thought of "*Deo volente.* . . ." ["God willing"]

Yes, but in terms of prayer, Mass, breakfast time, lunch, moments of work, visiting, what is a typical day like?

There is no typical day, but when we're at home, in Budapest, we normally have lunch at 1:00 because we eat together with our colleagues, and you have to have a schedule. We normally have dinner at 7:00, but there are so many liturgies, so many occasions, when we either do not have dinner at all or have it much later. Breakfast depends on the schedule of the Mass: whether we celebrate it in the morning, or if we have liturgical obligations during the day or the evening, and because of that, we are not celebrating the Mass in the morning. And then, there are even some national or semi-public liturgical or religious obligations, or funerals, or Masses offered for the repose of somebody, or in honor of some national holiday, or some commemoration that has been requested, or that seems appropriate at a given time. And of course, there are invitations, academic events, church events abroad, but also in other dioceses. For example, the last time, last Sunday, I was in Satu Mare, I was the main celebrant, I had to give the homily . . .

Where?

In Satu Mare, Romania, in Northern Transylvania, in honor of the beatification of the martyr bishop János Scheffler, which made a great impression upon me. The celebration was broadcast by several TV stations, then there were some interviews, then the bishops had already half-finished the lunch by the time I was able to free myself from the journalists. . . . Always like that. . . . So, it's no longer a question of my favorite dish, it doesn't matter!

How many times a year do you have to come to Rome?

It depends. This also depends on a thousand factors. When there is a convocation. Six, seven times, definitely, at minimum.

Six or seven times? And how many days each time?

It depends. When there is the synod, it lasts three weeks. For the past three years, I have been present at the synod, every autumn.

Then . . .

Meetings of European bishops. The CCEE (Council of the Bishops' Conferences of Europe). The plenary assembly is once a year, but other meetings, such as the "Joint Commission" with the CEC (Conference of European Churches), the umbrella group for the Protestant and other churches, then, periodic regional meetings, meetings with Catholic bishops of the Eastern Rite, the meeting of Southeastern Europe, sometimes I send a representative. So, six other occasions in general, making a total of up to fifteen. Then, sometimes I have to go to Brussels for the plenary session of COMECE (Commission of the Catholic Bishops' Conferences of the European Community). . . . Then, for example, in mid-June, I was in Brussels to celebrate a Holy Mass on the occasion of the end of the Hungarian presidency of the

European Union (2011). They invited me—it was not my idea, but I gladly accepted. The cathedral was full, thanks be to God; it was a beautiful moment.

Any personal meetings with Pope Benedict XVI?

Yes, they are always unforgettable.

But have you had longer discussions, more in-depth, for example about Europe?

We make a report, and we also ask for some guidelines. Every other year we make a type of *ad limina* visit with the Presidency of the CCEE. . . . We visit the Holy Father and then all the related dicasteries. This is also very interesting and substantive. In 2011, we also presented to the pope the records of the last Catholic-Orthodox Forum, on the relationship between Church and state.

CHAPTER 7

THE PRIVATE MAN

"The world is complicated, and this is the main challenge.
Because no one has the strength to engage with the details,
which actually would be necessary [for understanding]."

How MANY priests are there in Hungary?

Two thousand.

Diocesan and from religious orders?

Mostly diocesan. The members of religious orders are either
foreigners who come for two years of training and go, or are
elderly and already retired; there are few who are active,
and the ones who are are occupied with the duties of their
specific charism, not with pastoral duties.

And the greatest challenge that you are confronting now?

(Pauses) The multiplicity of challenges. (Laughs)

And how can you simplify this?

The world is complicated, and this is the main challenge.
Because no one has the strength to engage with the details,

which actually would be necessary [for understanding]. And in the modern world, this is the main problem.

That is why even the Holy See, when formulating magisterial documents, must have a large number of experts. For example, on an issue of bioethics, or the environment.

So the multiplicity of problems, the high level of complexity of today's world, can only be dealt with by a great bureaucratical apparatus. And that's a problem, but this is also a circumstance that encourages us to emphasize the international character of our Church.

We need all the other Catholic Churches—that is to say, all parts of the Church—and especially the teaching of the Holy See, because our own strength is not enough for the level of complexity of the new problems. We also have a need, a vital need, for the collaboration of scientists, lay people, experts from different fields in order to arrive at a moral conclusion in many situations.

What are the things that you like? Going to the mountains, or to a restaurant, or walking, or swimming?

Fresh air, taking walks in nature, definitely. Certainly more the mountains than the seaside. Usually, during the summer, it's too hot at the beach. For example, I really love the Italian coast, Capri, Ischia: in February, not August. Swimming as well, when my schedule permits.

And skiing?

I don't know how to ski; I never had the opportunity to learn how to ski.

Bicycle?

Yes, definitely. But now not so much.

Working in a garden?

I never have, we never had a garden. No, that's not true, because my grandparents had a second home close to the Danube, where there was a small garden and we each had a small piece of land where we grew some onions, some vegetables. It was when I was ten.

Do you keep a diary?

No, not at all.

No diary?

Nobody who grew up in the Communist world does such shocking things.

Music?

I love music.

Which composer?

I love Rachmaninoff, for example. I very much like the selection made by Don Giusanni, a number of pieces. As an instrument, I love the violin of the great violin masters such as Yehudi Menuhin. Certainly, I have often attended the opera. The national opera. I always used to go at least ten to twelve times each season. But not anymore.

And who do you like?

I like Verdi, I like the classics. Wagner is also very nice, but it sometimes seems too majestic. I would say that very modern music like Stockhausen is interesting to me, but it's not an everyday sort of fun. I love Hungarian folk music, and folk music of other nations as well. In my car, there is always some folk music.

And if you can speak of your close friends, who are they? The closest friend in your life?

I have friends from my youth who I can talk with, who I meet, if not regularly, relatively often. Among them are former classmates, then other neighbors. There are some intellectuals I know from university or met when we were organizing the Catholic university. For example, there is one who was founder of the Faculty of Information Technology, who is a truly multi-faceted man, who also plays several musical instruments and can sing very well. The genius for natural sciences and mathematics is coupled in him, as is so often the case, with the sense for music.

What's his name?

Yes, Tamás Roska, he's an academic (died in 2014). He is well-known, he's worked at Berkeley, also at Notre Dame. He has a son who is a priest. Then . . . some others. A jurist who is the dean of the Faculty of Law, an expert in constitutional law. He has a beautiful family.

And authors other than the Russians you like, who are they?

For example, to read Hermann Hesse in the original language is beautiful. It has a really rich, charming German.

And others?

Certainly Chesterton, Werfel, the authors of this type. But this is not only literature but also a manifestation of religious orientation. To tell the truth, I have read several translations into Hungarian of Spanish and American literature; that is, literature of Latin America such as Mario Vargas Llosa, for example. He does not appear, of course, to be a particularly Catholic thinker. His work is a bit surrealist, but always rich. There is always a direct experience of reality that attracts me. In the same style, but decades before, there was a writer from Transylvania who was a friend of my grandfather, Áron Tamási, who wrote the fantasy novels that I loved very much. He was not an overly religious man, but he also asked deeper questions about life, especially when he was older. He had a good sense of humor and a very enjoyable conversational style. Among the Americans whom I have read in recent times—almost by accident—I liked Chaim Potok and Isaac Bashevis Singer, the Nobel laureate who seems to have had a theological point of view while also dealing with more profane themes.

I asked before about your most joyful moment. May I ask you about a very sad moment in your life?

There were certainly sad moments when my parents died. My father died suddenly. My mother suffered with lung cancer for four years, heroically. I was teaching in Rome at the Gregorian and was beginning the students' final exams when I got the call from my sister: my mother is back in the hospital and very ill, and would like to see me. I took the first plane, which was the next morning, and I came home. From the airport, I went to the parish, where I lived; I left my suitcase and rushed over to the hospital. My sister came out of the room, already crying. Then I knew that my mother had already died. I entered the bedroom and she was alone in the room, on the bed. I felt [the pain] once more, like a punch, which is still present. I prayed there beside her body. After that, her presence was very strong for days, but there it was extremely strong, as if she had waited for me.

Then after five minutes, a friend of my mother comes in, a lady who was one of the mothers of these big families that I've mentioned. One of her grandchildren is now a priest in our diocese. She comes into the room and says, "She is still here." Of course, she knew that the body was still there, but she also felt the same impact of the spiritual presence of my mother. She's still here, she waited.

In our lives, these are experiences, not theological ones, perhaps natural ones, but they are windows. Our reality has a profundity that we do not fully understand. Sadness? Yes, sadness, because I came too late.

What did you want to say?

Nothing, I just wanted to see her. Especially in the end stages, talking too much is a waste of time.

So there is the ability to communicate without words?

Of course, embracing a sick person means more than a thousand words . . . or taking somebody by the hand, or making the sign of the cross on their forehead, or even just saying, "I love you, thank you for everything."

Another moment of sadness?

What is sadness? It's interesting. Pure sadness and pure joy are very rare things, I guess.

A moment of fear?

Fear . . . fear of sin, supernatural fear, exists on the one hand, but there is also earthly fear, for example, fear of authority. For example, I taught philosophy to a clandestine group of young people, but there was no fear. I knew that perhaps someone would denounce me. I asked myself if it was worth it or not. And I thought, these young people take in everything that I am telling them with so much interest, let's do it.

Has your life ever been in danger? A car accident or something else?

I haven't had any major accidents on the road. I once had a problem with my eye but I recovered, thank God. I am able to read, I can write, I can even drive a car. What else can I ask for?

Are there any very important passages in Scripture that have a special richness [for you]?

I love Holy Scripture in general. I can say that Saint Paul's hymn of love in Chapter 13 of his letter to the Corinthians was for at least six, seven years, if not ten, my daily morning prayer. Then, there are passages of Saint John, the High Priestly prayer of Jesus, or there are even passages from the Old Testament that strike me. Recently the two letters of Saint Peter, the tension that is found in these letters. That is to say, the word of God and the message of Christ does not have an easy time in this world. We are not talking about an organic development without resistance. It is a dramatic thing in history.

Is there a parable that has a special meaning?

So many. The first is the Good Samaritan, of course.

PART II

FAITH

Reflections on the Faith: From the Message
of Christ to the Life of the Church

CHAPTER 8

JESUS

"When we say Jesus Christ, this is the oldest
profession of the Christian faith."

WE BEGIN with Christ. What did "Jesus Christ" mean for
his contemporaries?

First of all, the term *Christ* is a historical and religious
expression, meaning Messiah. So, without [knowing
about] the expectation of the chosen people, without the
wishes and hopes of humanity, we cannot understand what
this word *Christ* meant to his contemporaries.

When we say *Jesus Christ*, this is the oldest profession of
the Christian faith. Of a known person, Jesus of Nazareth,
they claim that he is the *Christ*, he is the *Messiah*. So, it is a
profession of faith, which is hidden in this name.

And what does it mean to be the Messiah for the Jewish
people in Jesus's time? What did this mean for the people of
his time? Because of course there was no lack of those who
were waiting for a liberator, a great warrior who, by military
means, would fight for freedom, for the sovereignty of his
people, and so on.

Jesus Christ did not let the people make him king;
he actually went away when they tried to do this. He

considered his own mission to be the work of salvation. He wanted to save people *from sin*. So, without a correct, exact conception—which is also faithful to the mentality, to the understanding of that era—of *sin*, we cannot understand the role of Jesus Christ.

So, what does "sin" mean?

Sin in the biblical world is always about the relationship between man and God. So it has to do with this fundamental personal relationship.

The mission of Christ, the Messiah who saves mankind from sin, must be interpreted through the concept of "sin"? That is to say, the Messiah saves us from *what*? Do we need to be saved? Why? Is this concept still relevant today?

This is absolutely relevant. Now more than ever, because in this day and age, we appreciate freedom very much, but in what sense? So if there is a person who can free us, then it can be a great hope for all of us.

But what does it mean to be free?

So, it does not just mean something negative, it is not just to be free *from* oppression or *from* the bonds that prevent our advancement, *et cetera*, which is also true, but freedom also has a positive component. Being free means that we have the opportunity to develop the qualities within ourselves, to develop our mission, to seek and to bring about the reason for our existence: our happiness.

And how was Christ able, how is he able, to perform this role as a liberator?

First of all, I should say once again that this is not a polit-ical-military question, but rather a deeper question, more elemental, connected with human existence. If Jesus Christ were only a man, he could be a great sage, a great saint, he could be a philosopher, yet he would still be within this world, our world, which is full of problems. Therefore, he would not be able to break all that keeps us in bondage—not so much social but spiritual bondage—which requires a divine force, direct contact with that, which is the reposi-tory of the rationality of the world, the universe, and which knows everything about man.

And this is absolutely important because he knows bet-ter than we what will lead us to happiness. He knows, more than we can imagine, what is good for us. It's not that he's a kind of robot, where we insert the money, then we press the button and receive whatever we choose. No, he knows better what will serve our happiness.

But he was rejected in his time, crucified. It was also dif-ficult for Christians themselves to accept him because they wanted a political Messiah. The moment he said, "I'm going to Jerusalem to be crucified," they were gone. Then the second part of this rejection is the fact that after centuries and centuries of evangelization, the evangelized countries have also denied this faith in our time. How can you evaluate both things, that, in his time, he was not able to have success and that, after centuries, many have still refused this salvation?

I do not think he would have wanted to have another success, different from what happened, because otherwise, God would not be omnipotent. So, the divine plan has enabled this course of events and therefore the theology of the cross is an important element of our faith. Through the cross, through the stunning defeat, he triumphed. He triumphed more fully than he could have triumphed with any political victory in history. He even broke the dome of history and prepared a way for humanity, a way that leads to eternity, which is extraordinary.

You speak about this as an incredible and extraordinary thing, attractive, but many have denied, and again in recent decades, many have left this faith. How is it possible?

Leaving the faith, accepting the faith, these are not usually theatrical moments in the lives of individuals, and certainly not collective actions. There is, of course, an effect on society, especially when a number of believers, or non-believers, reaches a certain percentage, but there is growth and there is also frailty in all of us. Even those who followed Jesus wanted to leave him at certain times, and at the moment of death, even among the twelve many left him. Saint Peter denied him, after which he repented, he began to cry. So in the end, he remained faithful, in spite of everything.

So, there is a very open dynamism in all of us, open to good and to evil, to faith and to refusal, and so the rest of humanity lives this way. I would say that there is space, in fact, there is a need, for divine grace.

And this dynamism also responded to a widespread mentality in Judaism in the time of Jesus. The mystical reading of the Old Testament, the Bible of that time, which the Christians rediscovered, was already an existent reality. They began to read the Bible in a way that we also find in Philo of Alexandria and other authors, a way which for them was a great discovery; that is, that this had to happen, it was not an accident but was foreseen in the secret plan of God, that it was through this earthly defeat that the Messiah would have to triumph. This is outlined very well in the conversation on the road to Emmaus after the resurrection of Jesus.

To the disciples of Emmaus, Jesus himself declares and explains the meaning of the Scriptures from Moses through the prophets, shows that the Messiah had to suffer, had to bear this very thing. So there was already a context which at least allowed for the Christian explanation of what had happened to Jesus, and Jesus Christ had prepared his own followers, his friends, and his disciples for this.

This message, this reality, has been contested in all ages: the Romans persecuted Christians, then in our time Communists, also humanists, want to contest this belief, this faith. Does all this history make sense—all these decades, these centuries and centuries of the Church, the struggle to live this faith, to bear witness to this faith? And how long can it last? Can the Church's battle last for millions of years?

It can last only until the end of human history, as Benedict XVI said unforgettably, after the concert of Franz Liszt offered to him in Paul VI Hall in May 2011. As the psalm asks, *"Wie lange?"* "How long?" Of course, until the end of human history because God wants to walk with us, and since the redemption, also Jesus Christ wants to walk with us, he who has said, "I'll stay with you until the end of history."

But doesn't this journey seem to be sad?

This journey is very sad if we see it only through earthly eyes, because if history's only purpose is itself, or happiness is only an earthly condition in this, our life, then we are more miserable than all, as Saint Paul said. If we trust in Christ, only in this life are we the most miserable, in this world, because it is not Christians who become for their faith the richest, the most powerful, this is not the case. But simply because God exists, because God calls us personally to a friendship and a close relationship with himself, who is beyond time, beyond space, beyond the universe, this means that we poor terrestrial beings are called to participate in this eternity, personally. It is only through a relationship with God. So, this is the window that opens, this is the great freedom, and to fight for this or to announce this possibility to all in every generation is a beautiful thing.

And why is it so difficult to convince many people to see the beauty of this relationship with the transcendent God, the eternal God? Why do so many say, "No, I want to stay here with the pleasures and powers, and all the things of this world?"

First of all, because, to make an analogy, because the light of God is so strong, that our eyes are not sufficient to penetrate it. If we look at the universe, if we look at human existence with honesty, we will have a certain sense of the supernatural. But what is the world of God like? What is that level of reality that surpasses the cosmos like? We do not know, we cannot know about it through our abilities, our senses, and because of this, it is hard for us to even imagine it. The history of ideas about the afterlife, as it was imagined by different peoples, is a cultural history in itself.

This is the difficulty, because the other side is wonderful, but we do not see the details, and we cannot see the details. But the light from the afterlife reaches us. You can catch a glimpse of this light also looking at our universe, looking all together, with all of our being, from this side. And that means that if we renounce the other side, saying that we cannot know the details, fine, we don't know the details. . . . But can we then say that it doesn't exist? Or can we say that we are not interested?

Nowadays on television, they show so-called "scientific" movies that speak of vast forces, great connections in the "cosmos," the dangers, for example, that could threaten earth, and so on, which are interesting for everyone because from the unknown there comes something that can affect our lives here. Similarly, but on a higher level, so it is also with the world of God; there is something, some immense force that affects our lives even here, but we do not know about it, we learn about it only when the connection is made.

How is it possible that sometimes Christians fall and return again to sin and pride, or use the Church for worldly purposes? How is it possible that they do not bear witness to this God; in fact, they become obstacles to faith? How does it happen that Christians themselves become impediments

to seeing God, to seeing these eternal rays of light, that people say, "Well it's just another . . . ?"

. . . another ideology.

Another ideology?

So, first of all, the ancient Gnostic explanation does not hold water. The cause is not that material reality is inimical to spiritual reality, nor is it true that there are two gods, a good one that created the spirit and wants to save us, and the other an evil one who is master of the material world and who fights against light and against the spirit. This is not the Christian vision. We believe in one God, the Creator of all that exists. And that means that the possibility of sin, the resistance to the good news of the Gospel, or to the grace of God in general, stems precisely from being free, as sin is the decision of a free creature, and especially of us human beings.

So, let us return to the question of what is sin, and what are its consequences. Of course in the Old Testament, in the book of Genesis, we read of the fall of the first man, the original sin. Theology has developed this subject extensively. We profess with a clear consistency, even today, that Baptism frees us from many consequences of original sin. So, there exists something within us, which is due to the sin freely committed by intelligent creatures, human beings, and which makes it hard for us to find the way to God, to find an authentic connection to God. Saint Paul writes about this.

Our imperfection is also imperfection due to freedom,

or to the use of human freedom in a bad way. It resists the Good News, it resists genuine testimony to the good news of God, and of course, that may also obstruct the proclamation and the impact of the word of God in the world. It's true.

But it is also true that it is through the same weak human beings that Jesus wants to be present in history and wants to convey his good news. He trusted in the apostles, whom he knew, who were not great philosophers, who were not without their defects. Jesus understood that they would not be absolutely perfect, without any defect, even afterward. We know that Saint Paul rebukes Saint Peter for having been too conformist in Antioch. But soon after Saint Paul also calls for circumcision for his collaborator—who, theologically speaking, did not have to be circumcised because he was already Christian—simply out of respect for the people. And so he did practically the same thing for which he had rebuked Saint Peter earlier. The modern research then blends the history of Christian identity within Judaism and beyond it. There were, of course, those human aspects even in the great apostles, but through their testimony, which in the end was nevertheless still authentic and pure, the faith was passed down even to us.

Many people say that the Church has been a bad thing, that it has brought something that is not good to humanity, because it has brought wars, divisions. This is the argument that we often hear today.

Historically it is not true that the Church is the cause of the wars and the division. There was cruelty; there were wars

before it, too. In Europe, in the twentieth century the cru-
ellest things were committed in the name of anti-Christian
ideologies.

Better to have a faith of values without dogma, without reference to Christ. Have you heard this type of argument?

Yes, but I do not know many people who take it seriously,
because a faith of values without God, without Christ,
without the historical relationship between the divine reality and us, has no basis, it's too light. It's something that, at
least in this country, as far as I know, is perhaps not shared
by anyone. That is to say, the philosophical relativism of
values is one thing, but living without values is another
matter. The latter is very widespread, but it almost amounts
to the criminalization of society. It is not happiness.

No, but they say they are philosophical, but not religious. They want the values . . .

Yes, many in history have said this and all of them were
defeated. Precisely for this reason: because a purely philosophical theory has no basis in experience and does not have
any grounding in our historical reality. If the so-called values
are subjective and arbitrary, they coincide with our desires
and can lead to the struggle of all against all as a result.

We know of a society directed by such a philosophy,
which was Marxism. We do not dream, we do not think,
that this is the solution to humanity's problems. When the
official ideology is a non-religious philosophy, for us this is
not the current trend but rather something from the past,

which has proved unable to make people happy, or even to convince people, because all those who confessed it or propagated it were still unconvinced.

You speak of this faith in Jesus Christ. Can you say that you personally know Jesus Christ? If so, how?

To the extent that an ordinary mortal can usually know him, I believe I know him. Certainly, there are other opportunities in human existence to know him even more. The great mystical saints certainly have a much deeper knowledge of his person, but already the three ways of encounter with Jesus convey a true knowledge. And what are the three ways?

We see in the Gospel the disciples of Emmaus, in the Bible, learning, reading, praying, also looking at the exegesis of the whole Bible, the Old Testament, the New Testament.

Then, the community of the faithful, the Church, because they return to meet with the apostles, who say, "He is truly risen."

And the third way, the breaking of bread. When they eat together with Jesus, in that gesture, when he breaks a piece for them, they recognize him. Therefore, the Eucharist, the Mass, the sacraments.

CHAPTER 9

THE CHURCH

"This was the great discovery, that belonging to Christ,
belonging to the Church, goes beyond all other categories:
historical categories, human categories, categories of peoples,
of origins, because the Church of Christ unites all people."

"ONE"

So, LET's talk about the Church. In the Creed, we say that
the Church is "one, holy, catholic and apostolic." This is
the question: in what sense is it "one"? Especially when
there is division within the Catholic Church: division on
what part of doctrine to emphasize, and external division
with Protestants, with Orthodox, ecumenical issues. What
is the value of being "one"? How can you preserve this, or
work for this when there are divisions?

The original meaning of the unity of the Church, which
was professed by Saint Paul and also by the most ancient
Fathers of the Church, like Saint Ignatius of Antioch,
was very concrete; that is, that the Christians who came
from Judaism and those who had converted from paganism formed a single community and not two. This was the
original and concrete meaning of the unity of the Church.

The Jews and the Gentiles . . .

Exactly. This was the great discovery, that belonging to Christ, belonging to the Church, goes beyond all other categories—historical categories, human categories, categories of peoples, of origins—because the Church of Christ unites all people, the faith of Christ unites all people. And of course, this unity, in the course of history, has been placed in doubt due to other circumstances, and not only because of ethnic issues. The temptation toward ethnocentrism reemerges again and again in the Church, but there are also real confessional differences, differences in faith.

Yes, but usually it is said that by saying a creed, one comes into communion with all others who profess the same creed. Therefore, it becomes problematic when someone denies an article of the Creed. So, "one" because we are united in faith. If someone denies a part of the faith, he leaves this community.

The Church's unity is a *fact*; that is, the Church *is* one. All those who are baptized are members of the Church, if they are validly baptized. On the other hand, the Church is also visible. There are not two realities, the visible established Church and the invisible Church of grace. But they are two aspects of the same reality, as we are taught, following long tradition, even by the Second Vatican Council, among other things. Therefore, we must work hard to achieve an appearance of unity. Of course, when there are great differences in faith, we must keep in mind the old truth, which was emphasized also by the Second Vatican Council, that all Christians who are in communion with the Church of Rome regarding the profession of faith, the recognition of the sacraments, and the recognition of legitimate pastors are in full communion with the Church. The three criteria reiterated by Saint Robert Bellarmine. But the Church also teaches us that the Church of Christ subsists within the Catholic Church on earth. This means that the Catholic Church, which is a pilgrim on this earth, has no lack of substance, yet in terms of bearing witness to the world, the fact that there are also many of the baptized who are not in full communion constitutes a difficulty. So, full communion among the baptized is one of the main goals of our efforts. We must work and pray for the fullness of visible unity for the Church, for the unity of all Christians. This is not optional, we are obliged to want it.

I would like to talk about the interior of the Church and dialogue with those who are in another ecclesial community. Are there internal conflicts that destroy unity where there are progressives, traditionalists? How can we deal with different currents in the Church and keep them together? Maintain unity?

Speaking of unity, we cannot avoid the notion of communion, especially since the Second Vatican Council emphasizes this aspect so much.

Communion actually has several meanings. The most perfect communion is, of course, that of grace. If I lose the state of grace because I commit a mortal sin, now my spiritual communion is imperfect. When I was young, they taught us that one who lives in mortal sin is a dead limb of the Church. So, in order for spiritual communion to be perfect, even the state of grace is required. However, for full communion, which is a legal status as well, less is required; it takes those three criteria, of faith, of the sacraments, and of legitimate pastors. Even other differences can be legitimate: so, unity in plurality, for example, in the case of the Churches *sui iuris*, the ritual Churches; that is, the Catholics of the Eastern Rite. It is an asset that we have twenty-one of these Churches *sui iuris*, which have their own theological, spiritual, liturgical heritage, disciplinary as well. And it is a demonstration of the possibilities of the Church itself, of our faith, which can manifest itself in different cultures in different ways. On the other hand, there are of course also things that we do not consider matters of a legitimate plurality, because they are contrary to the fundamental truths of the faith.

And with the Orthodox?

With the Orthodox, the communion of which we speak, in the terminology of the Second Vatican Council, is very large, very broad. It is not yet, unfortunately, full, but it is almost full. There are many common beliefs. All sacraments are valid. This fact demands a great respect. We speak of the Orthodox as Churches. Many authors have written and spoken about the *Dominus Jesus* document, where the recognition of the Orthodox Churches as having the character of a Church has a special weight, because if we recognize that these Churches have all the valid sacraments but that their communities, entrusted to a bishop as their pastor, are of the Churches, it means that also the governing authority within these Churches is regarded by us, in principle, as legitimate. It means that we are able to recognize even many things from their own legislation.

How long will it be before we have unity?

How long it will take until full communion, of course, we cannot say, because I am convinced that full communion, if it comes, with our Orthodox brothers . . .

You are convinced?

I am convinced that this full communion, if it comes, will be a gift of the Holy Spirit; that is, not just the work of human beings. We must work and pray for that.

Humanly speaking, does it seem impossible?

Humanly speaking, creating the Church or creating full communion with another Christian community is, of course, impossible, because human forces are scarce, they are few. This is a matter of a reality that is on the level of grace.

How are the personal relationships with Patriarch Kirill of Moscow?

I would say that the Orthodox world is wide and the rest of us, here in Europe, must be in dialogue with all the Orthodox, autocephalous, and autonomous Churches, that live on our continent. Certainly, we have a very friendly relationship with the Ecumenical Patriarchate, we have a very important relationship with the Moscow Patriarchate, but also with the Patriarchate of Bucharest. And now even our relations with the Serbian and Bulgarian Patriarchates are becoming more active. So, these relationships develop gradually. The Catholic-Orthodox Forum is a network of relationships, it's a very beautiful dialogue, because there, all European Orthodox Churches are represented, and all the bishops' conferences of Europe.

Who has worked to put together this forum?

Many people have worked. I also have had the privilege to collaborate in the preparation of this. Certainly, Patriarch Bartholomew and then-Metropolitan Kirill, now Patriarch of Moscow, were positively active.

It seems to me that Kirill has spoken of the world today using a "political" analysis. Is this true?

Well, certainly a Russian thinker, a Russian intellectual, feels the responsibility of his own people even for the political fate of humanity, Russia being a very big country. They are also accustomed to thinking in global terms; that is, on a large scale. And so they see environmental problems, certainly, in Russia, these types of problems arise. They see the need for international cooperation for the solution of these problems because they no longer can do so much at the national level.

For example, against pollution, the contamination of the environment, no? Then there are other issues that, let us say, refer rather to human coexistence, or internal concerns of society. For example, the collapse of village life throughout almost all of Eastern Europe. In Russia, for example, this is a big problem, and also in Hungary. The depopulation of the villages for various reasons. I will tell you a few of these. Agriculture, whether in Russia or in Hungary, was fully collectivized to the point that farmers were no longer farmers but agricultural workers in a factory, and when agriculture was transformed after Communism, they did not return the land to the farmers. In Russia, perhaps they didn't even know who the owners were anymore, and they didn't know anymore how to farm the land. Even here there was this problem, that the older people still knew how, but the young people perhaps didn't know or didn't want to work any longer in agriculture, so the villages have been gradually abandoned. This is a problem.

Then there are of course issues related to the criminalization of society. This is a general challenge, and here I think that the Christian faith is truly a force. I am not saying directly, immediately, but through education, the values that enable a society to live truthfully without physical, concrete, and immediate compulsion can also be revived.

Then, with the Protestants, can we create a unity of faith?

Of course, the Protestant world is very wide. On one side there are the so-called historical Protestant Churches, although they are not called that by us, that come from the original reform of Luther, of Calvin. There are so-called evangelical communities, neo-Protestants, or even communities that are labeled as sects in different countries. I would say that with the historical communities there are structures for ecumenical dialogue that are established, well-known, and applied. Like the ecumenical week of prayer at the beginning of the year. Regular meetings. Then with the Holy See, there is an organized dialogue on theological issues.

However, it is also true what a cardinal competent in this matter once said, that some in these communities are beginning to move very quickly away from their own traditions and it is not technically possible to run after them. There is a tendency among some to be very conformist to the liberal or subjectivist public opinion of the Western world. This trend, of course, where it is very strong, does not facilitate dialogue.

On the other hand, with these Christian communities, there is a relationship, not only of mutual consideration, but of mutual respect. And there are forms of collaboration in different areas of life.

Now, with the evangelical community, sometimes there are problems because, if someone talks about us as the Antichrist, or is cursing us in the mass media, then it is hard to find the right voice for dialogue. Then it is also difficult when one partner has a systematic theology, and the other has certain effects, which sociologically fall under the category of charismatic phenomena. And still, even these communities have merits; that is, in these communities, there are many people who believe deeply, so not only because of social opportunities, not only because of cultural traditions, but also because of personal convictions. And among believers, there is also a level of possibility of comprehension. So, this new challenge and opportunity is not to be forgotten.

Among some of the initiatives to dialogue and pray together, one example was the day of prayer in Assisi in 1986, which was attended also by Pope Benedict XVI when he was Cardinal Ratzinger, even though as a cardinal he made some criticisms. Is it possible to distinguish between attempts to collaborate, to reach a mutual understanding, and at the same time to avoid a type of syncretism?

I see a substantial difference between the dialogue with Christians, which is ecumenical dialogue in the technical sense of the word, and a dialogue with non-Christian religions. Because with Christians, with certain limits, certainly, we can pray together, because we pray to the same God, in the name of the same Christ. We pray, as we hope, in the Holy Spirit. While with many other religions, we do not address the same God. So, praying together does not seem possible to me. Praying with the same intention or praying simultaneously, yes, it is possible. But not together.

ISLAM

How can one, from the perspective of the Church, judge Islam, the Islamic world, and the Western world's attitude toward this phenomenon considering also the peaceful invasion of Muslims into Europe, where it seems that within a few years there will be a danger of a certain political weight of this people?

Being in this city of Budapest, I cannot begin with anything other than a historical reference. During the Turkish period, which lasted 150 years in this country, the authorities never forced the population to convert to the Islamic religion. Of course they confiscated most of the churches; however, they never forced people to convert to Islam. In the Ottoman Empire, before the First World War, 37 percent of the population was still Christian. So, enlightened nationalism . . .

Returning to the original question about Islam, it must be said that in the West, we see signs of nervousness with regard to the presence of Islamic communities in Western countries. A nervousness that, according to the statistics on their proportion of the population, is unjustified. It is unjustified because the vast majority continues to be Christian or of Christian origin in those countries. So, it seems to us that the real reason for this fear is rather that many of these people have become uncertain in their own identity. If your identity is not certain, then the presence of a minority who is strong in their own identity can create fear or worries.

So I would think that a constructive fidelity to Christian roots, respectful toward the convictions of each individual, can help a lot to overcome these fears and concerns.

There are some countries in the West where some typical dress of some Muslim groups in the state schools is not allowed, but it is permitted in Catholic schools. Why not? If the nun, who teaches, also wears the habit of her own religious order. So, there are countries where this is the practice. The Catholic Church has some schools in the East. It has schools, where less than 2 percent of the students are Catholic. We have experience in contact with many peoples, with different religions.

"HOLY"

Let's talk a bit about the second word: *holy*. The holiness of the Church. When I speak about this, I don't want to influence your answer, but there is the moral, there is good and evil, right and wrong, and there is sin and penance. Might we think that the Church is no longer "holy" if Christians embrace immoral lifestyles? Have we become like the world? Are we true Christians? What does it mean to be "holy"?

The holiness of the Church means, first of all, that the Church has as its head Jesus Christ, who is the Holy, with capital letters, and certainly, that all Church members have been sanctified by Baptism. Therefore, Saint Paul sometimes calls the recipients of his letters "saints." And why not? All Christians are saints in this way and have the opportunity to free themselves from sin through the sacrament of penance, and to deepen their sanctification through the Eucharist, through prayer and the other sacraments.

And there are always the saints in the Church. Saints who are then canonized, now like the martyrs of the twentieth century. I think that holiness is present and originates from the heart of the Church. Of John Paul II, many, if not all, were convinced that he was not only an extraordinary man, a charismatic man, a man of great abilities, but that he was also a mirror of Christ, that he was holy. The crowd shouted "*santo subito*" ["a saint immediately"] because they had felt something that was beyond human capabilities.

So, there are saints in the Church that reflect this holiness. There is the possibility of sanctification, there is the fundamental fact of Baptism, and of course, there is also sin. But the sin of the members of the Church does not detract from the sanctity of the Church.

Let us say also that in the Christian tradition, echoed by Hans Urs von Balthasar, the Church was also spoken of as the "chaste harlot." That is, there is among the members of the Church also the element of sin, as the first generation of Christians already suffered because of this; certainly, Jesus rebuked the apostles. They suffered because of sin, they had to overcome situations that arose from sin, as we see when Saint Paul rebukes the individual communities.

If the Church remains faithful (and it will remain faithful because otherwise, it is not the Church) to the teaching of the Lord, then it must also be the voice of holiness. Even when perhaps various social classes do not share its ideals, which originate from a height, which is not thought about by many; ideals which are actually, on one hand, higher than our thoughts, and on the other, more intimate.

As Saint Augustine says, "*Superior supremo meo, interior intimo meo*" ("You were more inward than my innermost self and higher than my highest"). So, this ideal, that we have learned from Christ, is found in the most profound depths of the world and of our human nature, and beyond our highest human ideals. So we represent something of the deeper and higher reality, which responds. That is, we can contradict it, we can go a long way in distancing ourselves, in many ways, from these ideals. But the reality, sooner or later, responds. And I think that the members of the Church are not at all lost and that this ideal received from Christ is vibrant in the community of the Church, in spite of every sin, every problem and weakness.

"Catholic"

The word *catholic* seems to me to have to do with universality, which extends over time and space, and in reference to a precise location, which is Peter in Rome. How can the Church be catholic?

The Church is catholic.

It seems that some say, "We are American Catholics," or German Catholics, instead of, we are just Catholics, period. There is this nationalism, the national church has become even "We are Catholics of a certain parish, and here we are this kind of Catholic" . . .

During the Baroque period, in the theological debates of the time, many Catholic authors protested against the expression "Roman Catholic" that Protestants used to refer to the Catholics, saying that it already diminished them. It is enough just to say Catholic. Certainly, the successor of Saint Peter is a reference point, but not in the sense that the Roman Church as a particular church would be the one that we call Catholic.

On the other hand, where we recognize the presence of the reality of the Church, we also recognize to a certain extent the presence of catholicity, as emerges at times when talking with our Orthodox brothers. And some of them say, "But yes, you are *Roman* Catholics," and I say, I understand, as an Orthodox Christian holds himself to be a true Christian, he should also hold himself to be a Catholic because catholicity as a criterion is clearly in the profession of faith. However, even in the Catholic literature in ancient times often we speak of our Catholic faith as the orthodox faith. That is, Catholics and Orthodox, even in the current Roman Missal, the first canon, we pray for all Orthodox in the sense of "all those who have the true faith." So Catholic and Orthodox in many contexts seem to be almost synonymous expressions.

But it is true that catholicity signifies a universality, and that originally we were not just a portion, separated from a pre-existing union; we understand ourselves as the community founded by Christ, which has expanded and wishes to be true to its origins. Catholicity means also the presence of the totality of the richness of faith.

"Apostolic"

The word *apostolic*. We have spoken of one, holy, catholic, now apostolic. What does it mean?

The apostolicity means that we are founded on the apostles, as Saint Paul says, or even on Jesus Christ himself, who is the only foundation, and that no one can build another foundation. He says to Saint Peter, "You are a stone, and upon this, I will build my Church." Which means that Jesus, through the apostles, and especially through Saint Peter, wants to be the foundation of the whole Christian community, because we receive the faith through the apostles. Through them, we also receive grace because they sent their successors and introduced sacramental life in the communities, so from the Apostolic Church, from the Church of this first generation, descends all our reality.

Can it be lost?

Naturally, it cannot be lost because Jesus has given a number of promises and a number of tasks to his Church, to the apostles when he first sent them out to preach the Gospel. He said, "I will be with you every day until the end of the world," and he also said that the rock of Saint Peter will be the foundation of a Church, against which the gates of hell shall not prevail.

So, we are the bearers of Christ's promises and we are the vehicles for his project. And it is impossible for his project to fail because he is God Almighty. And if he wished this, if he wished to use the humble human ministry, then that also gives us the grace to carry out this mission. So apostolicity means, overall, of course, the apostolic succession; that is, the sacrament of ordination, episcopacy and the priesthood. For us it is something fundamental, essential for the Church, just to be able to call a community a Church in the full sense of the word, as the Magisterium teaches. And it also signifies a task. Even we, even now, are obliged to be apostles, to be sent by Christ, so the mission's task is urgent. And the Church, if it no longer concerned itself with the mission, would no longer be apostolic.

CHAPTER 10

THE SACRAMENTS

"More than beautiful, powerful, potent—
much greater than ourselves . . ."

BAPTISM

"Baptism is the first sacrament, the
door to all other sacraments."

BAPTISM IS the beginning of Christian life. Is it a ritual at the level of the community, an ontological event with real meaning, even if supernatural? What is it?

Baptism is the first sacrament, the door to all other sacraments, without which no other sacrament can be undertaken validly, the sacrament of rebirth, the forgiveness of sins, the sacrament in which we wear Christ himself upon us, the sacrament through which we become members of the Church, the sacrament by which we receive the state of grace, the sacrament which is administered on this earth only through ablution or immersion in water, and with the words prescribed by the Church. At the moment of death it is, however, also possible to receive all the effects of grace of

the sacrament; that is, baptism essentially through martyrdom for the faith or through one's wish—a concept which
is now well-known—which does not have to be a concrete
desire to be baptized as in the case of catechumens, but may
be an even more general desire to seek the true God and his
will, and to fulfill it, or to be in accordance with everything
that we have recognized about him. This is the teaching not
only of the Second Vatican Council in *Lumen Gentium*, but
that passage of *Lumen Gentium* also cites a source, which is
a document of the Holy Office that was formulated in the
1940s during an American debate about the correct explanation of baptism of desire.

And the tradition of the Church says the same thing.
When we speak the profession of faith in the Apostles'
Creed, we say that Jesus "descended into hell," there, he
made some proclamation, and among those to whom he
proclaimed, of course, there were the righteous ones of the
Old Testament, of human history, who had lived and died
before the arrival of Jesus or before the redemption made by
Jesus, and who through his salvific work, not independently
of it, had, from then on, an open path to eternal happiness.

**So we can imagine that the desire of all is to be close to
God and the Creator in the deepest and innermost heart
of all human beings?**

No, it is the desire of the righteous, the saints, those who
engage their will to seek God, not just an automatic desire,
a desire without a human act. Nor is it a set of human
actions; it is the totality of a conscious search, then also
a series of actions, because we must follow what we have

recognized to be the will of God, what we have recognized as, perhaps, the true Church of God. So, a personal commitment with freedom and volition.

Is it possible to imagine the salvation of all humanity?

No. Salvation, in the sense that Jesus Christ wanted to save everyone, we have of course in the New Testament that he wanted everyone to be saved, yet the possibility of eternal damnation is also part of our faith; that is, we do not have Christian religion at a reduced price, we are not in a fire sale at the end of the season. No, it is a serious matter, and the Church has always distinguished, regarding the history of the Old Testament, the saints, the righteous, and those who were not. And so the Christian Church has always venerated as holy people those who had died even before the death and resurrection of Christ, beginning with Saint John the Baptist, but also with others.

In Amsterdam, I have been in the church of Moses and Aaron, and there are also others, David, who were in the Christian calendar, so the righteous and the holy ones form a specific category. Of course, we do not know all of them by name, there must be many, there must also be people who followed, who lived after Christ, but who were not truly able to hear the Gospel and were not able to decide with clarity and awareness about their acceptance or rejection of the Gospel.

If we think of China, India, Africa, there are millions of people, at least in the past and perhaps even today, who are not baptized and have not even heard the Gospel, but can

we imagine that they give, I don't know, food to those who hunger?

Above all, it is not just some instinctive acts, but it is also about a search for God, undertaking a search for the truth. It is about our duty to follow what we have recognized as the truth. But we can also speak of children, infant deaths, as the Holy See in recent years teaches us that God's mercy is also upon them.

It is true, however, that in the modern post-conciliar age the idea has spread widely that, more or less, God is very charitable, that God will have mercy whether for Christians who commit sins or for the non-baptized. It seems that after the Council a type of thinking has become widespread that says that missionary work is not necessary.

In different eras various ideas become widespread. Regarding missionary work, Saint John Paul II has already given the authentic response to this. He spoke of evangelization as a duty of the Church—that is, the mercy of God—because this is the true expression of divine mercy, in general, though it does not mean that our eternal destiny is not dependent on our behavior. It is perhaps the most beautiful passage from Saint John when he says that those who do not believe are already condemned because they have rejected the Good News, they have rejected the truth, they have rejected the faith in Jesus Christ. So, the fact that there is a difference between human behavior and divine mercy does not mean that God wants to save us against our will, evidently.

I would add that, with regard to mercy, at a recent meeting some speaker espoused and refreshed the old theory of Origen (or attributed to him), *apocatastasis spanto*; namely, that in the end, God will be merciful even to those who are in hell, even to the wicked, and all will go to heaven and everyone will be happy.

Somebody said this. Immediately the president of the session had to say that not all the views expressed in this congregation correspond, of course, to the faith of the Catholic Church. But anyway, it would be an exaggeration to return to the idea already rejected in Christian antiquity by the universal Church.

Usually, after the birth, you go to baptize the child.

We should baptize the children of Christian parents soon after birth, as the code says. However, some, for very human reasons, for secondary reasons, put off the baptism saying, "Ah, now the godfather does not have time," or, "We still haven't been able to choose the church where we want to do the baptism." These things are ridiculous in comparison to the importance of Baptism itself. And [this custom] is not an error, it is something that the Christians of antiquity also followed, since the time of the apostles, who also baptized even small children. In the Apostolic Tradition, it is said explicitly that those children who are brought to the baptism, but who do not yet know how to speak, will nevertheless be baptized, but their parents must speak for them.

Why do we give a name?

This is not necessary, it is not the essence of Baptism. But it is a beautiful custom, a beautiful historical tradition to choose the name of a saint, who will be the patron saint and who will also be an example for the one being baptized, an example to follow. And we believe in the protection of the saints, in the help of the saints, because this is an important aspect of the communion of saints.

CONFIRMATION

"With Confirmation, we receive all the graces that are necessary for Christian life, for testimony, for the profession of faith, for life according to our faith, and thus the completeness of divine help."

Then we have a second sacrament.

The Confirmation.

Many skip it today, but they even skip Baptism.

But one cannot skip Baptism, because if one is not baptized, he cannot take any other sacrament.

In Europe, this is also being lost.

Yes, it is possible to not be baptized, but Baptism is a prerequisite for all other sacraments. Confirmation has been viewed by some in a somewhat superficial way already since the early 1930s. The Holy See has rejected a theory widespread among some pastors in Germany that for confirmation it is necessary to be older; that is, they considered Confirmation to be the conscious decision of the now-mature individual. Today some in the ministry say that Confirmation is the sacrament for mature people, for adults, not children, but this is not true.

First of all, the tradition of the early church was to administer Baptism and Confirmation, and indeed the Eucharist, as part of the liturgy of initiation, a tradition preserved in the Eastern Churches to this day. And the Latin Church also prescribes that when we baptize an adult, we must also confirm him or her immediately after. Therefore, it is clear that the two sacraments are closely linked with one another, and so it is not a matter of adulthood in the human sense. Then, in a symbolic sense, or in an analogous sense, we can say that with Confirmation, we receive all the graces that are necessary for Christian life, for testimony, for the profession of faith, for life according to our faith, and thus the completeness of divine help, certainly. But it does not mean that we have to be adults in the human sense; as Nicodemus said when he spoke of the rebirth, "But I cannot return to my mother's womb, I am now sixty years old." It certainly is not about that.

As for the so-called free decision, those who are baptized in childhood certainly are in need of Christian education and of the personal deepening of their faith, this is clear. In fact, it is even necessary to always renew the baptismal promises that we make, and also the faith, that we must always profess. At every Sunday Mass, we recite the profession of faith and all participants say it.

So, it is not true that there is only one solemn moment when we come of age and make a personal decision; we make our personal decision and it grows as we grow in the normal human anthropology; that is, day by day, always maturing and never-ending. Full maturity is the state of perfection. So we are always on the road and we must deepen our faith, and our commitment to Jesus Christ, and life presents new situations when we are put to the test. So, we can never say that we are perfect in our acceptance or in our following of Christ. And in that sense, I do not think it is appropriate to postpone Confirmation for too long.

Some say that if we confirm only those who attend church and are already eighteen, they will remain in the Church and continue to attend afterward. That's fine, but if we confirm people only when they are dying, then all will remain faithful. So it's an illusion, a statistical illusion, because what is important is that those who are baptized also receive the grace of the sacrament of Confirmation, even to aid them in the struggles of their youth. It is not a matter of rewarding people for good behavior or [requiring that they be old enough to make] a solemn decision.

When would be the right time for Confirmation?

I am very open. I believe the Eastern tradition to be correct; that is, immediately after Baptism, even for children. I also hold the universal law in the Latin Church that says the age of reason, so seven years, to be correct. Then, I also would allow for the possibility that the episcopal conferences may petition the Holy See to accept another age limit for their country.

The Hungarian Bishops' Conference in the '80s and '90s repeatedly called for the age to be set at twelve to fourteen years. And I agree that when this is practiced, it depends on many factors, on the school system, on the way of preparing young people for Confirmation. But after this, to say to one who attends church—if he or she asks for the sacrament—you cannot be confirmed, this would be extremely unfortunate, because there is an effect of grace, it is not just an award like the general scholastic awards, like a good book that is given to someone who studies well.

We take a second name.

Yes, it is a beautiful custom. The confirmation name.

Is it important?

It is not so important; that is, it does not affect the validity, the substance of the sacrament. But it is beautiful to have another patron saint, to have another example. Generally, as in the Latin Church, those who are confirmed, they themselves choose this saint. Sometimes they see that there are names in fashion, in the positive sense. The last time when I confirmed there were three or four boys who asked for the name John Paul. It's a beautiful thing. They learned about his life, admired him as a person, and they chose this name. Or there are even some girls who ask for the name Teresa of Calcutta, very good.

EUCHARIST

"The Eucharist is the source, it is also the culmination,

the apex of the whole mission of the Church, of the
whole life of the Church, of the whole liturgy."

The third sacrament . . .

Eucharist. Eucharist because in the rhythm of Christian
initiation you arrive at the Eucharist—that is, the full initiation of adults finishes with the Eucharist—in the same
liturgy, as Saturday night in the liturgy during the annual
Easter Vigil I administer these three sacraments of initiation for adults in the basilica of Budapest. There are always
several candidates, every year in our diocese about five
hundred adults are baptized; of course, not everyone in the
Easter liturgy, in various parishes, even in the university
parish, but thanks to God this movement exists. So, immediately after the confirmation, in the same Mass, they also
receive their first Communion.

And how can we think about the significance and impor-
tance of this sacrament?

This sacrament has, of course, different aspects, the celebra-
tory aspect as Holy Mass which is, on one hand, a sacrifice,
on the other hand, a meal. Always on the other side, there
is also the sacred presence that remains even after the Mass,
which we can and must preserve with veneration, with adoration, in the Blessed Sacrament. The Year of the Eucharist
declared by John Paul II was beautiful, as it encouraged the
adoration [of the sacrament].

As for the Holy Mass, whether it be the aspect of the

sacrifice or the aspect of the Lord's Supper, it is important, of course, that we celebrate Mass as required by the Holy Roman Church. There are different forms and different degrees of solemnity according to the occasion, according to the churches, many possibilities. I do not know of any great abuses in recent times in our diocese. Generally, the Mass is respected.

Jesus said, "Man does not live by bread alone, but by every word that proceeds from the mouth of God."

Yes, that is true. It is also true that he says, "He who eats my flesh will have life."

How can we understand the presence of Christ in this sacrament? And what does sacrament mean?

Sacrament means "mystery." *Misterion* in Greek, so it is already a translation into Latin, that not every ancient Latin version contains. Some retain the Greek word *misterion*, and this means many things: secret, then according to the definition of the Council of Trent, it is a sign of a sacred thing that brings grace and that was founded by Jesus Christ because it was necessary to find a criterion to distinguish the sacraments in the strict sense and the sacraments in the broad sense. Saint Augustine writes, "Many are the sacraments, who could enumerate all of them?" Because if there are all the holy signs, then the sacramental signs, then the sign of the cross, which should be respected? And which are different with respect to the seven sacraments in the technical sense of the word?

The bread is seen as human life; that is, symbolic of all food. Bread and wine as all that we must eat and drink; that is, as all that can nourish us, like the Israelites in the desert . . .

Certainly, the Eucharist is the first. The Last Supper was a Passover dinner, a Passover feast, there is no way around this. Without this, what happened would not have had so much meaning, so it is full of significance. We understand it in the context of that profound reality. Even the nature of sacrifice. Of course, the unleavened bread that the Latin Church uses is perhaps the most original shape. The Church of Rome was very Jewish, more Jewish than many other churches of the Mediterranean basin in the early days [of Christianity]. In some respects, we are close to a pre-Christian tradition in terms of the formality and many things. Of course you could say, you should say about the Eucharist, that the Vatican has emphasized the fact that the Eucharist is the source; it is also the culmination, the apex of the whole mission of the Church, of the whole life of the Church, of the whole liturgy, so it plays a central role in the faith and in the Christian liturgy.

Confession

*"Christ gave, he conferred the Holy Spirit on his apostles
so that they would have the power to forgive sins."*

**Then there is confession. Jesus came to do many things,
but it seems that above all else he came to forgive sins.**

Christ gave—he conferred—the Holy Spirit on his apostles
so that they would have the power to forgive sins. It is not
power in the sociological sense; it is an ontological power, it
is a power on the order of grace to forgive. To forgive how?
Forgive as an instrument [of God], but forgive saying the
words, "I forgive you, *ego te absolvo*," of course in the name
of God, the Holy Trinity. The role of the priest is quite
moving emotionally, as it is moving even in the Eucharist
when one speaks in the first person singular Jesus's words
"this is my body." How is this possible? Only by the power
of ordination.

And then it is moving . . .

For the priest . . .

For the priest?

. . . but also for the penitent, of course. Receiving the safety
of God's mercy and forgiveness of God is moving because
there is, of course, the perfect repentance, there is the possibility of asking God's forgiveness with full contrition and
receiving divine mercy even when one has no chance to go

to the sacrament of Penance. However, there will always remain the uncertainty of whether my repentance was truly perfect. The Church also, not only for disciplinary reasons, but to aid in the functioning of grace, asks of those who come to receive the Eucharist or other sacraments such as marriage, for example, or even Confirmation, if Confirmation is made after the first Communion and first confession, that they be freed from their mortal sins through the sacrament of Penance, and not only through an act of contrition.

HOLY ORDERS

"Without the holy ordination, there is no Church."

Then we come to the sacrament of Holy Orders, which imposes a different character upon man, almost another birth in a certain sense.

Yes, in a certain sense.

Can you reflect on the meaning of this sacrament?

Absolutely. There is the succession of the apostles, with the signs and the words provided by the Church from generation to generation. It is a necessary condition both for the permanence of the faith, as Saint Irenaeus of Lyons has written, as well as for the continuity of grace, so the ordination of bishops, the priestly ordination which depends on the episcopate or presbyterate, these certainly are constitutive for the Church. Without holy ordination, there is no Church because there is no Eucharist, and without the Eucharist, there is no Church, as the Magisterium teaches. And then, a community of baptized Christians that does not have the Eucharist, that does not have the sacrament of ordination, is not a Church in the full sense of the word but is a Christian community where elements of the fullness of being a Church are missing. And that is why it is so important to pray and work for the full communion of all Christians.

Celibacy, chastity, holiness in every way as a priest, how is this necessary, taking into account also the fact that in the East there is a tradition of married priests?

There is the tradition of married priests, but there is also the tradition of ordaining bishops chosen from the celibate priests. And there is also the tradition of monastic life, so the appreciation of the ideal of the chastity of celibacy is continuous in both East and West.

It is a value that goes back to the person of Jesus Christ. And this is important. We come to know the real Jesus Christ through the Gospels, through the New Testament, because if we know him, then we know that he had a celibate life, he had a life totally consecrated to God and he also recommended this chastity to those of his disciples who were able to understand.

At what point did he recommend this?

When he spoke of chastity, when he spoke of marriage, the disciples said, "But if it is so severe with marriage that one can not send away one's wife, then it is not worth it to get married." And Jesus said that there are some who willingly reject marriage for the sake of heaven, "those who are able to understand, let them understand."

Of course, for humans, it is simply not possible, but it is possible for God; that is, it requires the grace of God, special grace, even to recognize this as a personal vocation. I should add that between the apostolic mission, the episcopal and the priestly mission, and the celibate life there is an internal spiritual relationship.

Saint Paul speaks of this, about the recommendation of chastity in order to give oneself completely to this ministry and to not be divided. He says that this is not a commandment, but it is a recommendation which, although simply a recommendation, transmits a value, transmits a precious thing. And in the history of the Church we know the developments, we understand that even within the Catholic Church there are the oriental Churches, the Churches *sui iuris*, who also have married priests, who ordain married men, but even they have also celibate priests and the monastic life.

Marriage

> *"It was Leo the Wise, the Byzantine emperor, who first ordered that a marriage blessed by a priest and contracted with this ecclesiastical formality should be considered valid, and none other. So, it was the state that required, for legal certainty, a particular form."*

Then we come to the sacrament of marriage, which, it is said, is a great sign that arises out of, that represents, that has to do with, the love of Christ for his bride, the Church.

Yes, these are the words of Saint Paul, of course, and because of this, we believe marriage to be a sacrament founded by Jesus Christ. And precisely because of this, we say that taking the sacrament of marriage does not require a special additional act of will, it is enough [for two people] to want to marry according to the will of God; that is, with an open-ended commitment for life. And if we are Christians, if both parties are Christian, then this valid marriage between them will be a sacrament, because they, as baptized persons, represent Christ, represent the Church.

And so it is not necessary to wish especially even for this sacrament, but it is necessary to want a true marriage. And if the two are baptized, it will be a sacrament. The practice of the Church firmly considers since long centuries that a valid marriage between two non-Catholic Christians, perhaps two Protestants, is a sacrament.

It is the only sacrament which, in a sense, does not require any other person. Baptism can be done even by a layperson, in a moment of need, but the only sacrament that requires no other person, even if we go to a church before a priest, is marriage, because it is the sacrament between two people.

But I would add that the priestly blessing is an ancient tradition, a tradition which is particularly prominent in the Eastern Churches, and is an act that is also practiced in the matrimonial liturgy of the Latin Church.

I would say that the canonical form, of course, is a relatively recent development. At the Council of Trent, there was some uncertainty regarding the Church's authority to prescribe a canonical form, without which a marriage would be considered void. Some said that one thing was certain: that the Church had the right to agree upon legal impediments to marriage, so therefore, it could also speak of the impediment of clandestinity (*impedimentum clandestinitatis*). Others claimed that the Church had the authority to establish a form for the validity [of a marriage] regardless of the terminology. As a consequence, the canonical form was introduced gradually because they made the compulsory nature of this principle depend on its promulgation in different countries, and there were Tridentine territories and extra-Tridentine territories for many centuries. So, in order to know how to resolve all matrimonial cases, a great deal of competence in canon law was required.

With respect to a prescribed ecclesiastical form, it was Leo the Wise, the Byzantine emperor, who first prescribed that a marriage blessed by a priest and contracted with this ecclesiastical formality be considered valid, and nothing else. So, it was the state that, for juridical certainty, required a certain form for legality. Of course, it could make reference to the traditions of the Church, which practiced this [ecclesiastical ceremony]. In the ancient Church texts, in the Councils of the first millennium, there is not so much discussion about the validity of a marriage. This is the mentality of the second millennium. In the first millennium, the question was: in what marital or family status must a Christian live in order to be able to receive the sacraments?

And the answer?

It depended on the circumstances, on the history of the different societies. Because in Roman times, of course, there was no equality before the state. There were slaves, there were free people, there were masters, there were *sui iuris* people, there were people who were in the condition of *filius familias*. There were also diverse forms of marital or near-marital cohabitation, such as the traditional and solemn form of *confarreatio*.[1] Then there was also concubinage, which did not have the negative connotation that it has today, but which was a type of cohabitation below marriage, usually because the parties were of different social classes.

There is the modern trend, I do not know the social and cultural history well enough to know how it was in past centuries, but in modern times it is said, it is believed, that there has been a trend of divorce in recent decades.

Divorce in what sense? First, it was necessary to introduce civil marriage.

Which was not there before?

Of course, it was not. If a medieval church tribunal announced the divorce of the married parties (*Divortium*), then it either ordered separation, or it confirmed that the

---

1   In ancient Rome, confarreatio was a traditional patrician form of marriage. The ceremony involved the bride and bridegroom sharing a cake of spelt.

parties did not live in a valid marriage. Until the baroque
era in Europe, there was no civil marriage. States regarded
marriage as an affair of the Church. And the registry—that
is, the book of the marriages of the parish—was generally
prescribed only since the Council of Trent. So the main
difficulty was providing proof. For this reason, beginning in
the fourteenth century, it was necessary to make the marital
announcements, to announce the names of engaged couples who wanted to marry for many weeks and in all places
where they had spent at least six months after reaching
adulthood, because otherwise they might be considered to
be in a clandestine, an undeclared or non-legal, marriage.

Then, the canonical form was not required for validity.
For lawfulness in the late Middle Ages, but not yet for
validity [in the eyes of the Church]. So, it was possible that
someone might have already a wife or a husband in one village and wish to marry someone else in another village. So
they would have to wait, they would have to hear the news,
to see if anyone knew about the previous relationship, then
it would be necessary to clarify whether it was truly a marriage or something less. And after that, they could marry.

And the matrimonial protocols in the Middle Ages, in
the pre-Tridentine world, were not protocols for challeng-
ing the presumption of the validity of a publicly contracted
marriage, more often they were protocols for declaring the
existence, the validity, of an already existing clandestine
marriage. So, indirectly, they challenged the validity of
the subsequent marriage. We see legal pleadings in abundance. There has been scientific research encompassing
all of Western Europe. Charles Donahue, for example, at
Harvard University, has worked in the organization of this

research, and many others. So, it's a fascinating thing and we have a great deal of data.

But there are two poles. One pole is, shall we say, romantic, and the other pole, if we can synthesize it, is political. For this second pole, there is the example of Henry VIII, who wanted to divorce his wife because he felt another need which was very important for him: to have an heir. He could not have another wife, and he did not believe that this person, his first wife, would still be able to have a son, and he broke away from the Church in order to have this divorce. The Church said that the marriage was valid, but the Church was also saying this for political reasons . . . .

And also for theological reasons, because the appraiser who was entrusted with this case was Cardinal Tommaso de Vio Caetano (Cajetan), who was a great theologian and canonist. He had previously written a great deal about questions related to the sacraments. I would not think that he made a predominantly political decision, even if there was a great deal at stake politically, evidently, because Spain was involved, England was involved.

However, some argue that it might have been possible to reach a political and theological agreement to allow the divorce even in this case.

I have not studied that case in detail.

Then, on the other hand, there is a romantic aspect. One says, in the modern world, "I do not love my wife anymore, my wife does not love me anymore, and this is the midpoint of our lives, and it is an emotional ordeal to continue when feelings no longer exist." How can we understand this?

I, first of all, I would like to begin by saying that I do not believe the state of marriage today to be so bleak, because if we look at history we can see enormous problems also in other eras. We can talk about the beginnings of Christianity among the Germanic peoples. There was *Muntehe* and *Friedelehe*: two types of marriage. *Muntehe* was a more solemn marriage that was agreed upon by the two families, not by the two parties, so it was an alliance of two families that was stable, it was solemn, but it was not dependent on the personal will of either party.

Then there was *Friedelehe*, which had more to do with love, with the personal relationship, but which was not considered stable, which could be dissolved according to the pagan traditions of these Germanic peoples of that time, and the Church had a difficult mission in spreading the ideal of Christian marriage among these peoples.

Georges Duby wrote a beautiful monograph about the priest, the lady, and the knight, which is a history of the struggle of the Church to spread the ideal of Christian marriage among the highest social classes of the Franks. It was a long road and we cannot say that in ancient times everything was perfect.

Now, today, there are some advantages. One advantage is that all people in the modern world—I am not talking about more traditional areas—consider marriage to be a personal act. In fact, the majority of people want to enter into marriage because of personal love, and this is a very beautiful thing. This is positive, it is a sign that the individual is playing a greater role in our vision of marriage. There is also, however, a certain sentimental exaggeration.

Nowadays, not only with regard to marriage, there is a cult of the moment, of momentary well-being, of the "feeling." Some say that the only purpose of life is the "feeling," that I have to feel good right now, in this moment. This mentality, however, has some major flaws, because the human being has a higher calling: we can think about the past, about the future, about others; in other words, we can consider ourselves in the context of others. Therefore, momentary well-being does not meet all of our needs. Even on this earth, if we want to have greater happiness, we must feel important and valued with regard to our future, with regard to our relationships with others. So it is not true that the momentary feeling is everything. And for this, we are obligated to seek out meaning, to give value and meaning to life. And this [meaning] is true happiness, a greater happiness. As is written in the psalm which says, "You, Lord, have given us greater happiness in our hearts, greater than those who have wine and wheat in abundance."

And this is the point, that also for marriage it is not the momentary feeling that is decisive, but we must also be responsible, we must think about the future, we must make a stable commitment, which is also a greater form of love. I think this should be the road to developing a relationship. And I also think that many are not satisfied with the [mentality of] the moment, and they are also searching for these points of view.

As for divorce . . . Thirty years ago it was believed that

the biggest problem was divorce, because so many people divorce after a civil marriage, or many thought even that the biggest problem was that many of the baptized no longer are celebrating canonical marriage, only civil marriage, either because it is already their second marriage, or because they are no longer interested in the faith, or because they are not so confident in their relationship and are already thinking about the possibility of divorce. And in modern states divorce is generally possible, the divorce of the contract, of the institution, that the state defines as marriage. That which is contracted before the Church, that which we consider a sacrament, especially when there has already been cohabitation between the parties, is indissoluble. It does not depend on the judgment of any court: if it exists ontologically, it is valid, and it cannot be dissolved, even by the will of the parties. Actually, we consider the so-called marriage according to the natural law also as indissoluble if it was contracted according to the will of the Creator, even if either one or both of the parties were not Christian.

Isn't it true that many reach the age of twenty, twenty-five, even thirty years without the spiritual and mental maturity to be able to promise themselves for life?

I don't really believe in this so-called maturity. I've said that the process of maturing does not end, except with death. And so . . . perfect people able to make a mystical, fully mature decision . . . let's not exaggerate too much. This is not necessary, even for marriage. It takes a normal human being, who is already able to take on the duties of stable coexistence. It takes goodwill, it is not such an extremely, terribly serious decision.

Indeed, people of today are afraid of commitment, and also afraid of choosing a vocation or a profession, even. I know many students who leave one faculty and begin to study in another one and have already passed the age of thirty and still haven't finished even one diploma course.

That is what I was saying.

And this also relates to marriage. So, today it is not like thirty years ago, where the main problem was civil marriage or even civil divorce, but that many do not even want to have a civil marriage.

They do not want to make a decision.

They cohabitate, but we have statistics that say that the cohabitations outside of civil marriage are less stable than civil marriage cohabitations. And the canonical marriages between believers, between Christians, are still more stable, statistically. Unfortunately, even among faithful Catholics, it will happen that they request a civil divorce, sometimes they ask also for the declaration of nullity of the tribunal of the Church.

There are two mistaken attitudes. One is rather careless, which says that even though it is not a divorce, nevertheless, those who seriously request it will obtain a declaration of nullity. That is not true. Serious grounds are required for nullity; it is not that the decision of whether to declare nullity or something less is based only on the wish of the two parties. This is carelessness.

The other attitude is also sad, when one says, "Ah, it is not possible, once I have been married before the Church, I certainly will not receive any accommodation, so I will not even try, I will not even think back on the circumstances [of my marriage], but I will abandon religious practice and begin another life." This is hopelessness.

Before I spoke of the wave of divorce, saying that there seems to be 20, 30, 40, 50 percent . . .

Here sixty. In Hungary, 60 percent of civil marriages end in divorce.

This led me to begin this discussion, to see if there really are true marriages, if human beings who begin a marriage are capable, or if we are more attracted toward sin today than half a century ago, or if we are more careless?

These divorces are civil divorces. And civil law considers marriage differently; it does not regard marriage as an indissoluble bond, as a condition that applies until death. No, rather they consider it as a bond based on the duration of the mutual intention to be together, and that is why, when this will ends, they then declare a divorce. However, we believe marriage to be something else.

There are so many questions. If two people live separately, are they still married?

Yes.

But if they continue like this for years?

Even still.

Until death?

Yes.

And if they do not see one another?

Whether they see one another or do not see one another, they can even take the sacraments. If they do not remarry and do not live in an invalid, or extra-marital relationship, it is not the case that they should be hopeless, that they should distance themselves from the Church only because the marriage has broken down. We have to work pastorally with people.

Can it really be that a failed marriage remains valid?

Yes, because once it is entered into normally . . .

And how often does that happen?

I do not know. These relatively new titles of nullity, which were first used by the tribunals and later also appeared in the law, in the new code of 1983, incapacity to assume the marital obligations for psychological reasons, these are given out not because of the laxity of the courts, but because there may be many people who are so distracted and psychologically problematic who cannot take on these duties, and this inability may also be relative, like impotence. So, it is also possible that when somebody entered into a marriage with another person they were mentally incompetent, and years later with another person, they can be competent. But we must carefully examine all these cases. Laxity of the judges is unjustified.

Yes, because we could also speak about the priesthood, which remains until death, but there can be a failed priesthood in a certain sense, like a failed marriage. A priest who betrays . . .

There are priests who request laicization, who leave the priestly ministry. We have various statistics at the national and international level. In Hungary in recent years, in the new generations, that figure stays around 10 percent; if we also consider the previous decades, we can speak of 20 percent leaving. However, with 60 percent of marriages ending in divorce, we must say that priests still constitute a fairly stable and serious class of society.

What does divorce mean for children?

It is always terrible because children have a psychological need of a father and mother. When these two parties, the parents, no longer love one another, it's terrible, it's suffering for the children.

Can we order people to love one another?

No, but we can . . .

That is, can we command love?

. . . love is not just momentary well-being, it is not just a feeling. In the musical *Fiddler of the Roof,* what is it that the old people sing after decades of marriage? "You do not love me," sings one, "What do you mean I don't love you? I've worked for you all my life," the other one replies in the song. I think it is like this, love is not only a momentary feeling, it is a commitment.

Are you very romantic, or not?

Whichever you like.

What do you think when there is a marriage of two young people who love each other, and you know that there are very serious problems because work is hard to find and their salaries are not very high and the children will be an economic burden? You see people like these who get married because you sometimes have to preside at the wedding, right?

Yes.

Do you think these young people are brave?

All newlyweds are brave and have to be brave. Nothing is certain in this life. In today's world, everything is in motion, especially in those countries where the whole economic and societal system was turned upside down. And this general uncertainty seems to be the cause of the demographic collapse, which is especially brutal in these countries. We are more affected by this than the Western countries, which nevertheless also have this serious demographic problem.

It takes courage, it takes trust in Providence. When there were already five of us in the house, my parents said, "The apartment is already too small, but we have no money to buy another or to rent a bigger apartment." At that time, it was not easy, and my father said, "We must pray." And we prayed regularly for the solution to this problem. And eventually, someone from our circle of friends said, "I know a couple who have a larger apartment and now need to move." So we found the necessary apartment, so, there is also this.

But the Church can help families, couples in a more . . .

Not only can help, it is helping. Visiting all the parishes in the diocese I discover with great and deep joy that there are, in almost every parish or at least every second parish, communities of large families who assist one another. These communities meet in the parish and are brought together by their common faith and they read the Scriptures together, they talk about their problems, and when there is a practical problem, they are able to help each other.

Before, in the '50s, '60s, this phenomenon also existed but did not yet have a name. There weren't spirituality movements, but my parents knew many other families with many children, Catholic families. There was a priest, there were the so-called holy girls, who wanted to join religious orders but were not able to because the orders were banned, but they worked. They calculated the minimum amount that was necessary for them to live, and if they had any money above this minimum, they distributed it among these families. Then they visited families to help the mothers, if the mothers could not do all the housework, or they even watched the children while the mother went to the doctor or the store. It is very important to avoid the psychological burden of the young mothers who live at home with several children, who are at risk of losing all of their social contacts. This is a very encouraging fact.

In many dioceses, there are centers for helping families. In the latest years, counseling services were established for the remarried divorced, where on the basis of the personal history of the parties they are offered help, whether the situation can be legally corrected. In many places, they are organizing counseling for those who experience difficulties in their marriage. It is important that they receive help with a Catholic spirituality. The parishes and the dioceses organize programs also for the families, such as summer camps, baby and mommy clubs, et cetera.

It is something that every bishop and every priest should do.

They should help, because their main concern is the families themselves.

ANOINTING OF THE SICK

Then we come to the last sacrament.

The Anointing of the Sick.

What does it mean?

It is certainly a sacrament that was and is the subject of extensive historical research, both about the theological aspect and about the disciplinary and liturgical aspect. We have in the letter of Saint James the mention of this sacrament, we have the decision of the Council of Trent, we have the practice of the Church. We believe that this sacrament helps the patient in two ways: for healing, God willing, and also to make easier and more perfect his or her penance. Naturally, it does not replace the sacrament of Penance, but it also has an effect on the remission of sins and penalties because in Catholic theology there are different levels of consequences for sin, there is the *reatus penae, reatus culpae, et cetera*. We believe that even after death one can still undergo some type of punishment before arriving at the state of complete happiness. And the dying person also needs special grace to step over that threshold.

Certainly, the sacrament of Extreme Unction should not be trivialized. We cannot say that all of those who visit the sick in the hospital—for example, deacons, lay people who have permission to distribute Holy Communion—that since they are there, they can perhaps give the anointing of the sick. They cannot because it will not be valid.

And there have been a number of abuses in this regard that have been rejected by the Church. So, it is a sacrament that can be administered only by priests. You cannot simulate this sacrament; that is, use another oil, say other words, do something similar if a monk has come, or a nun, or a layperson, to visit a sick person, no. This would be a false-hood; the Church rejects the simulation of the sacrament.

We have a system of providing for the sick, here in Budapest. In Budapest, there are about eighty hospitals, and we have the great challenge of planning for the care of the individuals who need it.

Before the war, there were many chapels in hospitals and there was also an abundance of clergy and religious. We have now reestablished a central chaplaincy for all hospitals which is housed in a small church in the oncology clinic. It has a deacon, two priests, and then lay collaborators who have organized the spiritual first aid service for each hospital, so they know the phone number, if a Catholic patient needs spiritual assistance, they can direct the patient to this center. This center has organized and collected a list of priests who are ready to go visit the sick on certain days. So, anyone can say I accept three days a month, or one day a month.

You can make almost a computerized schedule.

Yes, there is a center. So, if a request comes from a certain hospital, the central chaplaincy knows who the closest priest is who is prepared to go, and lets the priest know. The priest goes, brings the sacraments, possibly also hears confession, gives sacramental absolution.

As for the other patients who are not dying, several things are done. There are lay representatives, who are instructed to distribute Holy Communion. Now in various hospitals, we have again a chapel where we preserve the Sacrament. It's a beautiful thing because the Sacrament itself, through its presence, does a great deal of the pastoral work. We have guest books in these chapels, and many patients write, even some doctors, some relatives, write unforgettable phrases, because they are in extreme situations and they pray. They are not desperate, but they are very worried. And when they are able to rely on the mercy of God, it's beautiful. It is a program that is going forward.

Of course, we also have the administration of the sacrament of the sick in private homes, when one is already very ill, when they call the priest. We also have, and this is a relatively new thing because it has existed as a possibility only for a few decades, the community administration of this sacrament in the parish churches. Usually on the day of the sick or near that day, with, of course, spiritual and theological preparation, with the possibility of personal confession, we give this sacrament.

Perhaps there is a tendency to forget that even today, in the regulation and theology of this sacrament, there is mention of a certain dangerous illness. Now, for those patients who are beginning to be in danger, meaning in danger of death, we do not need to be purists. However, this is not just a sacrament of the old, it is not a sacrament for all those who are above sixty years old. The pastoral approach, on the one hand, should not be to make it only a sacrament of the dying, but neither should it be a sacrament just of the elderly or retirees. Instead, it is a sacrament of the seriously ill, who are starting to be in danger. This pastoral aspect requires some sensitivity, but my experiences are positive. In most parishes, there is this communal form of administration of the sacrament, but they are also willing to visit the sick on certain days if there is an urgent need.

To conclude speaking about the sacraments, it seems that the Church, through the shepherds, the disciples of Christ, distributes the means, the channels, of divine life and of grace to human beings, from the moment of birth to the moment of death, and in the critical moments of life. The vocations of matrimony, of the service of God, the moments of coming near to God in the Eucharist, the moments of reconciliation with God in confession. How can you evaluate all this apparatus of sacraments, of modalities of grace? Is it a beautiful thing?

More than beautiful, powerful, potent—much greater than ourselves. Grace is truly at work, Christ is at work. The entire liturgy, but also in a special way the administration of the sacraments, is the action of Christ and of the whole Church.

When a society—Communist, atheist, or secularized, 100 percent humanistic—loses and no longer uses the sacraments? Or in the Soviet world, when it was very hard to find the sacraments, or even prevented?

Millions and millions of former Soviet citizens asked for and received baptism after the collapse of the system because they knew that their grandparents were still Christians. Membership in the Church is a force that persists for generations. It is not so easy to forget this.

As for the humanistic world, if only it were truly humanistic—instead I see indifference, not a serious pursuit of human values. Yet, even if human values were seriously investigated and pursued, they would be based only on human experience, which is of course far below what divine revelation can tell us. If there were a serious initiative to improve the lives of people (that would be positive) . . . but I see mostly indifference and resignation. In the environment of resignation, we require the Good News of Jesus Christ.

CHAPTER 11

FAITH, LOSS OF FAITH, FINDING THE FAITH AGAIN, AND TRUE FREEDOM

"Jesus Christ is present in his Church even today. Jesus Christ is near to us. We can become his friends."

DOESN'T FAITH in Christ, in the twenty-first century, seem like something very "old-fashioned"? How can we explain to the modern world the value, and the necessity, and the beauty of such a faith? Who is Christ, really?

Christ is the Savior and liberator of mankind, the Redeemer of man, of humanity, as Saint John Paul II has written; Christ is man and God, true man and true God. He is the window, the door, as he said. The only door through which we can enter, and therefore the center of history. The center and the end of history. He says that he will return and judge all of humanity at the end of history. Jesus Christ is present in his Church even today. Jesus Christ is near to us. We can become his friends. He used this word, speaking with his disciples. Even today we can approach Christ also by meditating on philosophical concepts, and when we speak of the divinity of Christ, often we must also clarify the question of what we mean by the word *God*. If one

hundred years ago the main tendency was toward a superficial kind of atheism or materialism, believing that beyond
matter there is nothing, or that so-called spiritual phenomena are only secondary, secondary products of the material
world, today the general temptation of our culture is no
longer this. Rather, because we no longer see the boundaries between matter, spirit, energy, there is a general global
uncertainty, connected with a trend of openness toward
any religion, toward the religious, the holy.

Perhaps the temptation of pantheism is stronger today,
and therefore acknowledging Jesus Christ as something
divine, something that goes beyond the visible world, seems
easy to many. But to recognize hidden power also in all
other things—or in other words, pantheism—is very risky,
and the Gnostic eras reappear again and again in history,
for if we believe all that exists to be divine, then nothing is
truly divine. If all of this world is divine, then why is the
dignity of man greater than the dignity of a piece of stone?

So can we speak of advancement, can we speak of being
superior, if everything is God? In this sense, reality is no
longer structured. That is the temptation. In the face of
this temptation, we have historical certainty. Christ is not
only a theological being, but Christ is Jesus Christ, that
person who was born in Israel, who was crucified under
Pontius Pilate, so already the profession of faith places him
within the historical chronology. Jesus Christ was an historical person. Not even his adversaries, not even those who
refused to recognize him as the Messiah, denied his existence, because he was a man of that time who was known.
It is this real man whom we affirm with faith as the Messiah, who is God and liberator.

Are there any authors who may be useful in today's world in order to understand, learn, and believe in all this? Who are the best ones?

First of all, Benedict XVI, who wrote his great book on Jesus of Nazareth.

What is special about this book? Why is it useful? Haven't all of these things already been said?

Novelty, in faith, is not a positive property. The research of the natural sciences in the modern world is always oriented toward discovering something new. In history, in theology, the logic must be a bit different, because with the historical reality of Jesus we are connected with the testimony of previous generations. The testimony accessible through historical methods. So, the relationship between the historical Jesus and the Christ of our faith, as many German authors noted already in the nineteenth century, this relationship is the salient point of the matter.

The Holy Father has touched the center of the problem, stating that we all believe that the historical Jesus is the Christ of our faith, is the same person, and that the Church has believed all that we believe about Christ, because this is what Jesus of Nazareth taught, this is how he acted, he died and rose again. So, in the life, in the history of this person, we have the basis of our conviction that recognizes in him the Messiah, and even God.

A Plan to Renew the Faith

"First of all, I wouldn't give up on reading and writing."

How would you design a program of renewed study for Christians, for Catholics?

First of all, I wouldn't give up on reading and writing. Some might say, "It's superfluous," because we have the audiovisual world, so why write? Why read when I can listen to everything, just by pressing the red button? But Jesus Christ left us also his teaching, which was then written down. He himself respected the Holy Scriptures, he read in the synagogue, he explained the Holy Scriptures, and so God wishes to communicate with humanity through human words, through the tradition of concrete texts like the Bible. And if for no other reason, simply because of that we must not give up on this knowledge.

We are not obliged to read the Holy Scriptures when we are twelve. We are not so much people of the book in this way, but at least the whole of the Church can carry this knowledge within itself. It was not for nothing that Charlemagne made the parish priests teach children to read and write. The Catholic school was prescribed by Charlemagne out of necessity, because it was the Church that had preserved this during the period of the collapse of ancient civilization, even in the West. So our task is to create islands of high quality, like Boethius in his time, no? With the Vivarium. These were monasteries with libraries, and they chose what absolutely had to be preserved from the inheritance of the ancient world. Or the great Saint Isidore of Seville, who through his encyclopedias saved what could be saved of the knowledge of the ancient world.

But if today we have these new technologies and we can access in two minutes the complete works of Saint Thomas Aquinas or Saint Augustine, what do we really need?

We need to know how to read. And we must have the concepts with which we can arrange the elements of knowledge, so we can truly reap the benefits.

MEMORY AND FAITH

"We do not need to rely completely on computer memory; we must have our memory."

Who can teach and read?

A good teacher, who understands things himself. He must also have a lot of remembered knowledge. We do not need to rely completely on computer memory; we must have our own memory. They say that the geniuses, the great scientists like Albert Einstein, had a brain structure which easily allowed for the exchange between different parts of the brain, and so associations or connections, for them, were easier. But that is only possible if we have something in our brains. If we have some content, then we can make creative associations.

But perhaps we should then outline a curriculum and which things to memorize. Can we think about making some attempt in this direction, in proposing to the Church a renewal of studies?

We must start with catechesis, I think, before taking on the teaching of mathematics. At least catechesis. In Hungary, we are now, for the first time since World War II, able to publish a book of religion for each grade in the school. Actually, one of my sisters, who is a professor of pedagogy, directed this project, which I'll show you. (Stood up and went to get a book in his study.) These are the religious books for the first eight grades of primary school.

And this is even on the internet, so for the children, it is very popular now. Then we have the *Compendium of the Catechism of the Catholic Church*. We have a common base for all. But returning to the culture, the cultural project, I know that in America, in some centers, it has become fashionable to read the most famous authors. Maybe Saint Augustine or Saint Thomas Aquinas; in other words, directly to the source. I like that and I appreciate it, but I would make a small observation. Here I see a certain danger of fundamentalism. Because before reading the great authors, we must have categories, so first one needs to take a systematic course on dogmatic theology, and then in the scientific seminary we can say, "This year we will read this work of Saint Augustine," or, "Next year will be this work of Saint Thomas." Without a systematic course of patrology, reading two texts, two Fathers of the Church, is very little, because we cannot put what we read in context. So, institutional courses and working with the sources.

I want to bring out another response. We do not, as Christians, share the view of the philosophers that we have to be smart or educated to be saved. Do we have to be teachers?

No, it's not that. Not all Christians must be teachers, but the Church must be a teacher even at the highest level of human knowledge because the Church is in dialogue with the whole of humanity.

With respect to mercy and spiritual life, can we also think of a renewal?

I see certain signs of renewal because today people love to move. They love pilgrimages. The World Youth Day (WYD), for example, what a surprise! Never before in history have there been so many young people coming together to pray, to sing, to participate in the liturgy. The catecheses that are done are a great thing. Someone of my generation might think, "Well, it's too much of a spectacle, maybe now they feel some emotion, then later they will forget it all." I have also thought like this. But I look at the seminary, I see among the priests many young people who received their vocation during a WYD meeting, and they have already done priestly service for several years. So, it was not just a fleeting impression; it is a sign.

Or the pilgrimage to Compostela, which is now world famous. Or in Hungary itself. In the year 2006, which is also an important anniversary (the fiftieth of the revolution of 1956), we recognized two national shrines, which were traditionally two ancient sites of pilgrimage. By declaring these two national shrines, we have created the basis for further development. And we see this development.

Reflecting on the Council

*"It seems as if it was a new universe after
the Council that was born . . ."*

**But where to take, in a global sense, the result of the
Council, bearing in mind that no one knows what would
have happened had it not taken place? How can we judge
it today, fifty years later? As a necessary thing, a positive
thing, really a new springtime in the Church, or an almost
total confusion?**

No, I think neither one nor the other. It seems that it was
a necessary and providential thing, and the total confusion
touches all of civilization. It is not something specific to the
Church; even though in the Church different signs of ero-
sion began to be seen after the Council chronologically, it
is not clear, on the one hand, that they were a consequence
of it. On the other hand, we can make the comparison once
again with the Council of Trent. Even that one began to
produce its various fruits after several decades. As a biblio-
phile, I consider also the effects of the Council on books,
on the official books, used as a basis by the Church. And if
we take a look, after the Council of Trent, its decrees were
published. Fine. Then also the Catechism, the Roman Missal, the Roman Breviary, then they did an official edition of
the Bible, the Sistine or, more precisely, Sisto-Clementine
Vulgate, which served as the basis of Catholic theological
work for centuries. Then with all of these tools, they also
made the reform of canon law. The Gregorian edition of
the *Corpus Juris Canonici:* the Corpus was revised in light of

the Council of Trent. And the new edition was published for the first time in 1582, whereas the Bible was published only at the end of the sixteenth century.

So, I think that something similar happened after the Second Vatican Council. We have the texts of the Council. We have the *Catechism of the Catholic Church*, in fact, we have also the extract, the *Compendium of the Catechism*, we have the new liturgical books, although they are sometimes still not published in a practical form. These small details of the Roman ritual, which today are not all in one book; they are a bit complicated when in use. However, all or nearly all of them were published at least in the typical Roman edition in Latin, because the translations into languages, like ours, have not all been completed yet. The Missal, of course. But, for example, the Lectionaries, the last volume of the Lectionary came out a little while ago, then also the Bible, the Neo-Vulgate, then the new Latin code, then the Eastern code, then the reform of the Roman Curia. John Paul II asked that we have a new *Corpus Juris Canonici* [Code of Canon Law, 1983 ; Code of Canons of the Eastern Churches, 1990; and *Pastor Bonus*].

So, it seems as if it was a new universe after the Council that was born. Of course finishing touches or other improvements are always possible, even the edition of the Vulgate, the Clementine edition, was slightly modified two to three times; in other words, it wasn't simply printed and then left absolutely untouched for two centuries. However, most of the work seems to me to be done. And we have to digest it and turn it into practice in the whole Church. I am sure that the Holy Spirit, who directed the Council and development of the following decades, will not abandon us on this way.

CHAPTER 12

LAW AND CHRISTIAN LIFE

"The law must respond to reality."

IN CANON law, the code of 1983 replaced that of 1917. Was it an improvement for the life of the Church?

But we cannot make comparisons this way.

But it is a step forward, wiser, more charitable?

This is not the issue. "Applicable or not applicable?" "Does it respond to the current circumstances or not?" The law must respond to reality because it is created to influence reality. The social reality, of course. So if a law speaks of things that do not exist, of course, it will not be effective. The problem was that between the Council and the [publishing of the 1983] Code many were uncertain. They said, "Ah, the old Code is not in effect anymore." Which was not true; however, the law had been modified so many times and it was complicated to work with, so many lost hope of figuring out the law that was in force at that time. And in place of this a fairly clear summary was published, which contained the bulk of the legal material, contained almost all the institutional and disciplinary innovations proposed by the Second Vatican Council, and so it was definitely a step of stability and of courage to say, "Enough with the unnecessary labor and prevarication."

What is the main change of attitude toward this canon law? What are one or two points?

Compared to what?

To the prior law.

Of 1917?

Yes.

Ah, first of all, in the 1917 code there was a great deal of discussion about benefices and other things that virtually no longer exist today. So that is why I say that it was necessary to bear in mind the current situation of the Church and the world, but it is also true that in the post-conciliar code there was also a strong trend, which in itself was not bad, even positive, to use also the results of the development of general or secular legal culture. The law of the Church generally has always taken some of the legal culture of the environment, already going back to Roman times, and even in the nineteenth century.

Do developments in the right direction truly exist?

The very fact of the 1917 codification was an influence in the Western world, where the law began to be codified.

We talked before about the Hungarian Constitution

being written so late. But this is nothing compared to the Civil Code because Hungary had its first Civil Code in the 1960s. Of course, there were different laws, but there was no Civil Code, and so the Holy See was quicker in the process of codification. As a technical tool, it helped in finding which field of law to apply. In this sense, I would say that the promulgation of the code was a step toward stabilization, although, due to the influence of the general legal culture, the private law perspective, or the protection of so-called private interest, now seems exaggerated to me. So the public interest is not sufficiently protected in different situations. Then the universal law of the Church often is based on the reality of the typical local church in Italy or Western Europe, where the Church still has economic means, and still has personnel with good education and formation, whereas in other countries, in the majority of the world, this is not the case. So, to make a diocesan tribunal function well, in accordance with all the regulations, this requires an economic and cultural effort. If it works well, if the conditions are right, it is an elegant and beautiful thing. But if the conditions are not there?

And the penal law, for example. There the criticism is, nowadays, very widespread. Many say that we need to review that part of the code because it is not effective enough. There is too much protection of private interest.

An example?

First of all, there are central canons that say, "The ecclesiastical authority, even when there is a legal precept, does not have to punish the one who committed the crime, if it sees another pastoral solution," *et cetera*. But this introduces an element of uncertainty, of great uncertainty, in the system, and certainly later on, for these scandalous cases of the last decade, they have had to introduce other norms through pontifical letters, through instructions of the Congregation for the Doctrine of the Faith, in order to make the penal procedure more effective, at least for some serious crimes, because the system was not effective enough. It protected the guilty ones too much. Who protects, who defends the public interest, the salvation of souls? This is the central point.

If the apparatus is weak, then at least the law must provide some stronger protection. For example, if all the rules are observed, the average diocesan curia in the world would go crazy. They cannot do all that work. They have no time for the daily pastoral work because they have to deal with all these procedures. We must radically simplify many formalities of the procedure because the institutional forces are lacking.

We need to make another reform of canon law?

I wouldn't say that. There are already reforms—that is, standards of execution, norms of implementation of the code—so not a radical change in the text, because for a code of the Catholic Church it takes thirty years until it manages to really start to affect the practice. Because we need to print it, distribute the text, translate it into so many languages, we need to introduce it in our instruction, we need to organize continuing education courses for the priests, for the ministers of tribunals and of diocesan offices, *et cetera*, in order to put it into practice. We have had this experience here in Hungary.

I had the honor of translating the code into Hungarian. We worked hard in order to also have a manual, to introduce everything in the instruction. Thirty years. This is the rhythm. So I would prefer not to make big changes.

CHAPTER 13

THE LITURGY

*"It's a beautiful work, very beautiful, demanding, preaching
the Gospel in the light taken from the Old Testament."*

WE'VE SPOKEN about the Council, about canon law, and
we left out for a moment the new liturgy of Paul VI. Some
believe that what the Council said about the need to translate the Mass into the vernacular was later exaggerated,
even distorted . . .

The Council did not prescribe this.

I mean, that the Latin language was to be privileged, but
that the Mass needed to be celebrated in a way that people
could understand it better. But, instead of just translating
it, they rewrote it entirely and changed the entire lectionary . . .

For centuries, of course, the Mass readings for each day
had remained unvarying. All the books of homilies were
based on the pericopes in the lectionary.

In 1750 and 1910, the Gospel for each Sunday was the same . . .

. . . or almost equally the sermons of Saint Bernard.

So the same Gospel was read on the same Sunday each year?

Yes, roughly.

So, it seems to me there was a loss of communion through the ages when this changed.

In so far as the substance is concerned, the continuity has remained because the same passages, or almost the same, still figure today in the Lectionary, but not always on the same Sunday, or only in one year of the three-year liturgical cycle of readings. But it would be enough to have a list of pericopes to show that the passage for this Sunday corresponds to the passage for another Sunday according to the old Missal.

Yes, but this is very complicated. It seems better to me to have an annual cycle that repeats itself.

Yes, the three-year cycle. On one hand, it has a long history, on the other, the history seems too complicated. The old sermon books from the baroque era, but even before, contained three sermons for each Sunday. Why? Because saying the same thing every year was boring. This is what many great homiletic authors thought. The Scripture passage stayed the same, but they chose different homilies to comment on the same passage. So there was a history.

Another issue is doing the two readings, or two lessons, one from the Old Testament, the other from the New Testament. Whereas before, even in the Western Church, it was done as it is done among the Orthodox, as it is done in the East, in other words, the Epistle and the Gospel. The Old Testament was rather neglected, just a few passages from the Old Testament were read in the Mass. So people were not very familiar with the Old Testament, it is true. Perhaps because of the need for more in-depth knowledge, in order to be able to explain and understand well, correctly and rightly, in a Christian way, the passages of the Old Testament, because since the beginning of the Church there was debate about the validity of the old law. If it is not valid as law, what is its value? Why can we, and why should we, read it at a Christian gathering? They read it, but how did they read it? They said that of course there are the prophecies. Then there are the fundamental texts from the history of salvation. Then there are the passages where events from the history of salvation of the New Testament appear already in prefigured form. This is of course already a very nuanced thing, if we are trying to explain the Old Testament in this way. And certainly, the texts, which in the original context sound like laws, no longer seemed like and no longer were mandatory laws, even on the moral level, whereas other moral precepts were considered mandatory. Like the Ten Commandments, no? So, because of all these preconditions [for understanding], they preferred to read a passage from a letter of Saint Paul and other New Testament passages.

I believe the rediscovery of the Old Testament is a positive thing, but I also see that there are few priests or theologians who can explain these texts well. It is a beautiful work, very beautiful, demanding, preaching the Gospel in the light taken from the Old Testament. It is possible if passages are chosen with wisdom and intelligence.

Maybe a little *vademecum* [handbook] would be useful, a book that explains to all the priests how to interpret.

And above all we would need a table, which appears in many printed editions of the Catechism of the Council of Trent, and which showed, for each Sunday or for each holy day of obligation, the numbers of the Catechism that can be explained based on the Gospel or the Scripture texts that were read on that day. Because the Code of Canon Law prescribes two things also. On one hand, in the homily of the Sunday Mass, we must speak about the texts that have been read in the liturgy, so it is a homily, not a free discourse about any topic, but a homily.

On the other hand, we must, in the course of the three-year cycle at least, explain all the mysteries of salvation, all of the important content of our faith. But how can we do this? Certainly, we would need to compose some tables according to the Gospels, or the Scripture readings of each Sunday, indicating which parts of the *Catechism of the Catholic Church* may be explained using which Gospel or which reading. It is an easy thing, a small technical thing, but we must do it.[2]

---

2   The Holy See published such a table of correspondences between Scripture passages read at Mass and passages in the *Catechism* in December 2014.

PART III

THE WORLD

The Crisis of Modernity: How the Christian
Faith Responds to the Challenges of Modern
Communism and Secular Humanism

CHAPTER 14

EUROPE

*"Europe is an old idea, a cultural concept. It's
something much bigger than the European Union.
Today there is a mistaken tendency to identify this
political entity with the cultural Europe."*

WILL THIS Europe, which is being built, be the end of
Christian Europe? Can the new secular humanist Europe
be reconciled with…

These designations are inappropriate. I cannot imagine that
Europe, as such, would be secularized or associated with
any concrete ideology. Let me tell you a story: During the
Communist time, a Hungarian priest, who is now a bishop,
went to France. With great difficulty, he had received permission to make such a trip. At the French border, the
French, with much suspicion, searched all of his bags. He
lost his temper and said, "This is outrageous! At home, I
am suspected because I am a priest. Here I am suspected
because I am from a socialist country. But we Hungarians
are not all Communists!"

So, to label a system, or a country, as secular or Communist or I don't know what, it's something where we are
probably referring to some public structure. And there are

human persons, who can think in a thousand different ways. Also, Europe is an old idea, it's a cultural concept. It's something much bigger than the European Union. Today there is a mistaken tendency to identify this political entity with the cultural Europe.

But maybe we're at the end of this historical period, that of different nations. . .

I don't think so, I don't think so. Nations—which are not to be identified in a simplistic way with states—are natural entities, while these structures are artificial so far, so we shall see how they mature in the future, from which sources they will nurture, what will be the historical vocation they will take up.

TURKEY IN EUROPE?

Can this Europe be extended? Can Turkey be part of it?

I think that the dynamism of the expansion or the territorial extension is not as strong as it was many years ago. Also because everyone can see now, in both old and new member countries, the difficulties of integration or the profound differences, and the Schengen borders have been closed. If anything, inside there are several issues or difficulties that would certainly grow if the EU were to allow many other countries also to enter.

Then again, formally and legally the promises that have been made to Turkey should compel the EU, when the criteria are met, to pursue the opening.

Islam in Europe?

But can Europe also integrate millions of Muslims?

What does integration mean? In Europe, millions and millions of people from other continents have been integrated. Whether Muslims, believers or non-believers, it doesn't matter that much. Integration means respect for the laws, first of all, in the country that one has come to, then, respect for the institutions, more or less. We should not expect more than that, in other words, total assimilation shouldn't be a goal, because each person, indeed each community, has the right to preserve their own culture, their own religion, their own language, and so on. So integration and assimilation are not the same thing. Integration is a policy that can be the goal. Assimilation is an exaggerated demand; if somebody wants those who arrive to forget their cuisine, their native language, their culture . . . why forget, if it is valuable? Everyone has the right to cultivate this.

Russia in Europe?

Is Russia part of Europe?

Russia is the bearer of a considerable part of European culture and history, of Western history. For Europe, in the cultural and substantial sense of the word, it is very important that Russia rediscovers its own cultural roots, Christian roots, *et cetera*. And they're working on it even now. And then, of course, a peaceful relationship, a relationship of collaboration, this is very important, but in this sense, even the United States belongs to Europe because they share a similar culture or the same culture, in a form specifically developed in their own country, no?

Many speak of the challenge of anthropology; namely, that in today's world a philosophy is being created of man as a random product of the universe, which can be molded a great deal, which can also be genetically modified. And they spoke also in the past of different types of men. There was *homo Sovieticus*, there was . . .

But this is just a play on words. They were men like everyone else, but of course, because of the social circumstances of a country, people can assume different habits.

What habits?

For example, if you cannot get involved in politics, then you will be oriented more toward private life. Or, if you cannot undertake certain personal initiatives, cultural initiatives, then you may become more passive. These things certainly . . . but not a genetic thing, absolutely not. And the same so-called Soviet men in Israel, in America, in different parts of the world, have turned out to be very active, energetic people. They have had a lot of success even in Russia itself recently, as we can see.

THE QUESTION OF MAN

Then, in the Europe of today, at the center of the debate, there is the question of humanity. There is a problem.

There is a crisis in the conception. What is a human being, and what value does it have?

Certainly. This is one of the main aspects of the crisis, and not only the philosophical approach, or in how we think about the human being, but in what the human being actually is. Perhaps there, in the reality, in the essence, in human existence there are changes underway. In other words, logical thinking, conceptual thinking, the culture of the word, or of speech, the culture of writing text. These things are in crisis because there is a great deal of competition from audiovisual culture. With electronic media, we can see images, maps, even plants, anything that we are interested in. We see many things before being able to talk about them, before having to talk about them. But if we don't talk about them, the concepts are less strong, less clear. This is an interesting question: using media, using our audiovisual capabilities, using our sense for symbols, for feelings, perhaps more strongly. But on the other hand not forgetting, not abandoning the values of conceptual culture. I think that, in this process, the danger is distraction. If someone has five phone calls simultaneously, then they are looking at the screen, this type of distraction does not allow us to think, to reason very often, and that would be a loss.

GENETIC MANIPULATION

You've spoken about genetic manipulation. I would say that the possibilities of modern biology, biotechnology, are truly broad. There is, on the one hand, the standard of respect for the human being, for the human person, for its dignity. On the other side, we have experience in something else much older, [a field] which was unfamiliar with these technologies, but nevertheless knew the rules of genetics. For example, in the breeding of livestock, [or] there were dogs or cats of a very pure breed, very refined, because it was sought after, or there were some very sought-after qualities in horses in Hungary, where there is a great tradition of horse breeding. And everyone knew that these valuable breeds, which had been produced by generations and generations of breeding, for the sake of a few important properties they had been made very vulnerable, very susceptible to illness, even just a change in their environment, they could not really withstand it. So, having some very excellent quality often also means that you risk not having other qualities that may be important for survival if circumstances change. And this is just a trivial risk, we are not yet at the philosophical level. When it comes to the human being, the utmost responsibility is required!

POPE BENEDICT AND EUROPE

Did the Holy Father (Pope Benedict XVI) have certain interests concerning Europe during this period?

Certainly. He is a great European.

What are these interests? What are the first specific points?

Not specific points; this would be too much because even the reality of Europe changes daily. Giving five specific points would be naïve.

But what are some guidelines?

Of course, we have to defend Christian values, we must bear witness to the central human values, because those values that we recognize in the light of our faith are not linked only to a specific culture. They are universal values, which are present in Europe, but also on any other continent.

But, examples?

Freedom, in the positive sense; that is, not in the negative sense of rejection of all engagements or all relations, but in the positive sense of being able to develop God's project, our abilities, et cetera.

Then the transmission of faith. One example: here in Hungary we wanted to produce a series of books for catechesis, the teaching of religion for all grades of the school, then we translated a manual of dogmatic theology for the seminaries, and also for the theology faculty, because it was necessary to have something modern and Catholic with clear content.

How do you evaluate the way in which Christianity can make an impact in the coming decades of the twenty-first century? And who can be attractive in putting forward the message of Christ?

It is Christ himself who is attractive because all of us need him and we feel this need, even if all of us do not express it in that way. So, if we can faithfully transmit his person and his message, then we will be attractive.

As for Orthodoxy, and not only Orthodoxy but Eastern Christianity as a whole, including the Catholic or the Eastern Rite Churches, I would say that there is something in their heritage that responds very well to the modern, or even post-modern, mentality. Precisely because we live in an audiovisual world, the liturgy, the aesthetic appearance of Eastern religion is something that touches the hearts of so many people also in the West: the icons, the music of the Eastern Churches, many things, and also the aesthetic quality of the liturgy itself, or even the sacred atmosphere of the Eastern churches.

All these things are important, and they are also close to the heritage of the Latin Church. Even in our own past, in our tradition, in our places of worship, we can find a certain aesthetic and very sacred element which can be attractive, which can also have this function. Certainly, as I've said before, we cannot renounce logic and the verbal transmission of the true message either.

You spoke of a cultural shift in information, that there is a culture of emotion, images, audiovisual symbols, entertainment culture, and that this is different from the previous culture, which was a culture of the word, of reading, of discussion. We are going more and more toward this new culture that perhaps is changing man himself or changing the way he perceives reality or the way in which he communicates with others. Can you reflect on this change that is occurring in front of our eyes?

Of course, there were and there are changes in man himself, in the anthropological reality of man. But these changes are not essential to history; we hope very much that man does not cease to be man. There is freedom and intellect, which will accompany us until the end of history because we are created in God's image. This similarity to God is evident in our freedom, our intellectual capacity, and also in the vocation to eternal life. But within this basic anthropological fact, some shifts are possible, such as the transition from a verbal culture, which was the culture before the spread of writing. And this process was slow because first, it was necessary to invent writing, then it spread through society very slowly. Charlemagne himself could not write; he only knew how to read, but he valued books very highly.

Then also the majority of the adult population in the nineteenth century was still illiterate; for example, in our country, it was in the second half of the nineteenth century that almost everybody began to know how to write and read. So we see this also in various poorer countries around the world, that the radio, for example, plays an irreplaceable role in ministry and evangelization, also for this reason.

But to return to the topic of the new changes, now audiovisuality and also the role of symbols, symbolic expression, seems again to be gaining space, having a wider reach, because symbols have an emotional impact that is very great, much more intense than a sentence or a word.

On the other hand, they are imprecise, so with symbols, people can also be greatly manipulated. Therefore, how we work with symbols is important, and the Church has a great history in this regard, simply because from the beginning we have had our symbols, from the beginning we have used the great symbols of the liturgy, and in fact, when it comes to these sacraments, they are not only symbols, but they are efficacious signs of grace.

So I think it is also necessary for our ecclesiastical work, for our missionary work, to employ our age-old symbols intelligently and incisively. The administration of the sacraments and the celebration of the liturgy must also be charged with this expressive power. So we have to foster and nurture more fully the sacred character of the celebration, the atmosphere of the celebration, the symbolic expression, but also always keeping in mind our heritage of teaching that goes back to Jesus Christ himself.

CHAPTER 15

THE THREE MODERN IDEOLOGIES

RECENT POPES have spoken of the "challenges of ideologies." We can speak of three great modern ideologies. One is Marxism, another is Darwinism, and the third is Freudianism. The great writers on the class struggle; that is, Marx. On evolution, the continuous development, say, of the universe, through randomness, Darwin. The third, Freud, the prophet of the subconscious, [saying] that we are moved by thoughts that we are not even conscious of and that we are, in this sense, without guilt because we are, in a sense, moved by forces of which we are not even aware, that push us toward, I don't know, sin, toward our desires. So, these are three streams of ideologies that seem to challenge the fundamental principles of the Church, of Christianity. Have you studied or reflected on these currents, or on others?

I have not found these three currents to pose large problems. Since high school, we had good, religious professors, who also presented the issue of evolution as a matter of natural science, not as an ideological issue. And of course, to make our faith in God depend on our understanding of the history of the material world, this would already be an ideological exaggeration. And so we did not have this problem.

This is a problem which is very pronounced in America, where a certain Protestant fundamentalism is constantly in confrontation with ideological liberalism. With us it is not like that. Even our theological formation was much more refined, much more scientific. And so it took into account the history of the literature, the methodology of reading and explaining the Bible. With regard to Freud, Freud was not very well-known in Hungary in my time. Before the war, yes, the Freudian school also existed in Hungary, but we did not believe or have much interest in such things.

Marx was not even an option because nobody believed in Marxism, so the challenges were different. The challenge [for us] was not thinking, being indifferent, or apathetic, superficially materialistic. Every ideal, every sincere and profound thought was welcome.

Does that mean that these thoughts are not serious, that they are just frivolous?

No, they still have importance, even if there is some exaggeration. We can, on the basis of limited experience, create a great theory that is then justified by up to 10 percent. And in the name of that, we can commit many crimes. Of course, yes. But theories are born in the West, and in the name of those theories, the bulk of the crimes are committed in Eastern Europe, Latin America, et cetera. It was always like this. It is the eternal dynamic between center and periphery.

In the Middle Ages, there was a saying among lawyers, who said, "*Leges in Italia feruntur, in Germania disputantur, in Austria dispensatur, in Hungaria non valent.*" And that meant, in a very technical and precise way, that the laws of the Roman legal system did not apply in Hungary because it was not a country under Roman law.

CHAPTER 16

THE CASE OF HUNGARY

"We are not a bridge, we are a ferry; in other words, we belong to neither one nor the other."

WE THINK of Hungary as a country between East and West, a bridge country, to some extent, and also a bridge to the Middle East and Turkey and the Islamic world. Hungary's role in this regard can be very interesting.

This is why the writers from one hundred years ago—for example, Endre Ady, the great Hungarian poet—wrote that we are not the bridge, we are a ferry; in other words, we belong to neither one nor the other.

But do you feel this personally?

I personally do not feel anything [like this]; I want to do my service. I do not create any ideologies based on the historical inclinations of different regions. This would be speculation, in my opinion, too poetic. But it is true that the routes, the geography are the way they are. The routes go through our country, we have historical relations with many peoples, we have also a fairly resilient mentality based on our historical experiences that perhaps can help us in understanding various others and various other opinions.

History of Hungary

I wanted to talk about the Hungarian nation. Did you feel Hungarian as a young person and, of course, today as the primate of the Hungarian Church? What does it mean to be Hungarian?

This is a topic that has been discussed constantly in the press of our country throughout the last one hundred years. The discussion is based on the fact that [the nature of] this people is determined by diverse cultural and anthropological factors and there is no consensus as to what these factors are.

But are the Hungarian people an ethnic group?

Yes and no. First of all, when I was young, I did not feel Hungarian. I was glad to live, I knew I was Hungarian, but to be Hungarian, what does that mean? We knew about the language differences. Then, I was very interested in maps. In high school, for a period, I even wanted to become a cartographer. So I was interested in political geography. I also read about history, I learned a little about international history, with very little reference to Hungarian history, because that was how the official materials [that were published] at that time were written. But during the Communist era, the education system in our country did not put much emphasis on the fact of being Hungarian. Yet it was no secret, there was one point that everyone felt was a bit delicate, that outside the borders there were some other Hungarian communities, living here and there. Then there is also the Hungarian emigration to the Western world. In the official books, very little was said about this, but we listened to, for example, "Voice of America" and other radio programs. When I was a schoolboy, there was also a half hour when I would search on the radio for "Voice of America" so we could be a bit informed. All this, and even Tirana, to hear a Maoist voice. This was how one began to orient oneself in the world.

Tirana, Albania?

Yes, because the Chinese had this voice there when there were some tensions between Maoism and the Soviet Union.

So, there are two factors. There is the ethnic factor, the historical memory of the people, and there is also the ideological factor.

Or the political factor, the daily politics. Of course, the simple fact that, in the paternal line, our family comes from territory that is in present-day Romania, makes this subject very topical. But my grandparents were not nostalgic; they were very realistic, especially my paternal grandfather, who had been born in Bucharest as a citizen still of the Habsburg Monarchy—so in the kingdom before Romania, before World War I—as a foreigner, the son of a man who had a small commercial business. They lived there and also had a school that used Hungarian as the language of instruction, which I was able to visit a few years ago. That building still exists.

But in 1916 . . .

In Bucharest?

In Bucharest, when the war broke out between the Monarchy and Romania, Romania changed sides in the war.

To which side?

To become an ally of the Entente powers.

Yes, a bit of a betrayal?

I would not necessarily put it that way, because it could also be considered as just a realistic step, but in the end, foreign nationals had to leave the country. So my grandfather and his two sisters moved to Budapest, already during the First World War. After the war, many others came, also from Transylvania.

My grandmother, however, did not; she remained in her village near Oradea, which is in Romania but near the border with Hungary, a beautiful city. And they were there, my grandfather together with his relatives who came from there, on holiday near Oradea in the '20s, and so he met my grandmother, who moved to Budapest only after the war to marry him. My grandmother did not have to go as a refugee to Hungary; she came for her marriage.

So what does it mean to be Hungarian?

So, the greatest Hungarian, this is a title that belongs to a unique figure in Hungarian history, the Count István Széchenyi, who was an economic and political theorist of the nineteenth century, more moderate than Lajos Kossuth, and who did a great deal of work for the culture and the economy of the country. He helped to build, for example, the Széchenyi Chain Bridge, which is the oldest permanent bridge over the Danube. Then he founded the Academy of Sciences, and he organized a national campaign to regulate the Danube, to ensure that it was made navigable all the way to the Black Sea. Very practical things. However, he also wrote a great deal. He said that the nation lives in its language. At home, he probably preferred to speak German, like many members of the aristocracy, but the fact is that this is a cardinal element of Hungarian identity, because all the other elements are very different.

First of all, there is the true history, that the Hungarians arrived over 1,100 years ago in the Carpathian Basin already politically organized as a people, as a political-military alliance of seven tribes that occupied this area.

And who was Attila?

Attila was the Prince of the Huns.

Four centuries before?

Yes, correct.

455, I think, was . . .

The Hungarians, I believe, came in 896.

But Attila made it all the way to France?

Yes, certainly. That people, the Huns, in some respects, had some kinship linguistically, or even in their customs and material culture, with certain groups within these alliances of Hungarian tribes. But there is not a *sic et simpliciter* [pure and simple] shared identity between the Huns and Hungarians, which is something that has been of course a bit accentuated and romanticized in history, tying the two together. Then there were the Avars, another Turkic people of Central Asia, who established themselves here in the Carpathian Basin before the time of Charlemagne and who were defeated by Charlemagne, as we can read in the chronicle of Eginardo, Einhardus, "Vita Karoli," so those were the Avars. Then there was another wave of a people, who were called the Late [Late-Coming] Avars, who came in the ninth century, and previously, some Hungarians of Transylvania and the Szekely (Siculians) were considered by some to be descendants of that wave, of the Late Avars; in other words, of a people a bit more Turkic than average Hungarians, but a people that was nevertheless in kinship with the Hungarians.

But were the Hungarians considered a Turkic people, or not?

The Hungarians, as I was saying, were already an alliance of seven tribes. Among these tribes there were also ethnic differences; perhaps the language was already, if not the same, at least very similar between these tribes. In addition to the seven tribes, other peoples, other groups were already present in the Carpathian Basin, or they accompanied the Hungarians, like the Kavar or Kabar, another tribe in addition to the seven tribes, whose memorial can be seen on the Square of Heroes; do you know that monument in Budapest? If you don't, we can go see it.

They were a group who were not Germans and were not Slavs . . .

It goes a bit deeper than that. The memory of this early history is preserved in the language, and by now mostly in the language, especially in the language, though the Byzantine and Arab historical sources and some others tell us a bit about the journey of the Hungarians, beginning about the fourth and fifth century AD. We have information about the fact that Hungarians, or people who later called themselves Hungarians, because in the Byzantine terminology, they had another name, these groups lived within the context, or the organization, of the empire of the Khazars in the North Caucasus.

And the Khazars had converted to . . .

Judaism.

Judaism.

At least the ruling class.

So then there is a connection between the Hungarians and the Khazars?

Yes, because the Hungarians were living in that empire. They were one of the integrated peoples, or subject peoples, if you will, of that empire, which was a half-nomadic empire, especially in the steppes of Eastern Europe.

So, say, in the Ukrainian part?

Even up to Kazakhstan.

Even Kazakhstan?

Yes, southern Russia. In that area, down to the Caucasus. And they [the Khazars] made a strong contribution to Hungarian culture because various techniques, even terminology regarding military and state organization or administration, come from that era. In fact [there are] some words, some concepts of the Christian faith as well, because some groups in that empire were Christian. Constantine Porphyrogenitus even writes that Saints Cyril and Methodius had to translate the liturgical texts, the Bible, into Slavonic because a Slavonic translation did not exist, while for the Turks, for the Hungarians, for the Turkoi [Turkic peoples], there was already this text. Probably some groups of Hungarians had already encountered Christianity at that time, and some of the words in our Christian terminology date back to that era, but above all, other areas of life were marked by that experience.

Then we come to Saint Stephen.

Between Saint Stephen and the Khazar Empire, there is a fairly long time because the Hungarians broke away from

that empire. Then came the alliance of those tribes who had
their own prince, though its organization was according
to Turkic customs. Even the way of organizing the army,
the material culture, the organizational culture, was Turkic, while the language, in considerable part, in terms of
the fundamental structures, was Finno-Ugric. The Finno-
Ugric languages are part of the Ural-Altaic group of languages. So, if someone says that our language is related
even to Japanese, they are telling the truth, even if in a
limited sense, because the population of Eastern Europe
before the arrival of Indo-European peoples was Finno-
Ugric. This is why from Hungary up to Finland, to the
Urals, to Estonia, to eastern Russia, where there are small
groups of Finno-Ugric peoples, some other nationalities—
today there are seven or eight remaining peoples within this
family, but they are small nations, they are the remains of a
dispersed population, which was nevertheless a population
that covered the whole of Eastern Europe before the arrival
of the Indo-Europeans.

**I did not know this history; I knew just a bit about the
Celts, who were in the center west, and were pushed more
and more to the west by the wave of Germanic and Gothic
tribes, and who finally ended up in Ireland.**

Yes, perhaps the Hungarians were the first Finno-Ugric
group who arrived in the Carpathian Basin. However, they
arrived together with other peoples of Turkic origin.

**And then comes the great moment of encounter with the
Mediterranean peoples, the Greeks and the Romans. It**

can be said, beginning with Trajan and the conquest by Rome . . .

Do you see the problem? We can analyze the history of this land, of the peoples and cultures of this land, or the history of the Hungarians, which is a different history. The interesting part, the ancient part of the history of the Hungarians played itself out outside of modern-day Hungary, evidently. At the last moment—that is, in the ninth century—they enter the Carpathian Basin and more or less occupy this land, which was sparsely populated. There was not a dense or very organized population. And from here they made their expeditions, generally paid expeditions, as emissaries, called upon by various Western princes, because one would call the Hungarians to fight against some other one.

In this way, the Hungarians entered even the Iberian Peninsula, a few times they were also in Italy, but those were military ventures. They also reached Constantinople and made the Byzantine emperor pay them. Two of their princes were baptized in Constantinople, and one even brought a missionary bishop to Transylvania from Constantinople, Hierotheos, who has now been canonized together with Saint Stephen, because Saint Stephen's mother was the daughter of the Hungarian prince of Transylvania, who summoned this missionary bishop.

So far, we've spoken of the Hungarians who were beginning to come from the East.

But there is also the history of Hungary, of this land, of the people who lived here. We know that since the Neolithic Period, it was inhabited, with some agriculture, even in the time before written records. Then, we know that in the Roman era, in the beginning of the Roman era, the inhabitants, at least in the western part of the country, were the Pannonians, who were a Celtic people.

The descendants of these Pannonians were found, according to anthropological researchers, on the basis of the cemeteries, in some villages in the south-west of the country. They are still found there and speak an ancient dialect of Slovenian, which means that some of these Pannonians were definitely Romanized, others later became Slavs; in other words, they adopted a Slavic language, but we are talking about a not very dense population. Throughout this period, the Romans certainly already were cultivating wine. In Pannonia, they had some cities. Christianity, in the territory of our city here (Budapest), dates back to the second century.

The early Christians were among the Romans and came from Syria; perhaps a few groups arrived along with the military troops. However, we know rather little about the Christian hierarchy of Pannonia during Roman times. We do not have the complete picture of the bishoprics or of the metropoli, if there were any. But in Pécs, for example, in the south of the country, there are Christian catacombs, so there was already Christian history prior to the Hungarians. According to today's researchers, there was a Christian bishop's See in the territory of Budapest since the early fourth century. Then there were missions in the time of the Frankish empire, the Archbishop of Salzburg, especially, had a missionary vocation to the East. And this is shown by some churches that carry the title of Saint Emmeram, which were founded by missionaries from Salzburg in that time.

Even to the south of Lake Balaton, there is, for example, a church like this, and we have information about that mission. Also, there were some foundations from that period in what is currently Slovakia; for example, in the city of Nitra. Later, perhaps also as a result of the mission of Saints Cyril and Methodius, who came through Pannonia, some groups of Slavs were converted to Christianity.

Shortly thereafter, then, came the Hungarians, some of whom perhaps were already Christians. Over a sixty-year period, they began to better integrate themselves into the landscape of the peoples of this region. Especially after the defeat against the Germans in 955, they looked for ways of engaging, integrating themselves into the Western world; even though the Byzantine missionaries were invited, and came here, the majority of the missionary work was done by missionaries coming from the West.

The father of Saint Stephen, Grand Prince Géza, who had his seat at the city of Esztergom, near the Danube River, invited priests of Passau, which was an obvious thing to do at that time, because the main road was the Danube, the river, and from Passau on the Danube one comes to Esztergom.

Then there were the Slavic missionaries, especially Saint Adalbert, who has now given his name to the Saint Adalbert Center in Esztergom. Saint Adalbert was the bishop of Prague, but he resigned two times because he had to escape from the city, and even he himself perhaps did not know if the pope had accepted his resignation or not. However, he spent some time in Rome, and he also traveled across Hungary, stopping, according to our sources, our traditions, in Esztergom, where he carried out some missionary activities. Some say that he was the first bishop of Esztergom, but others say that he perhaps had the role of a missionary bishop, without a fixed seat, or that he was a bishop, but not an archbishop.

During the Humanist period (fifteenth to sxteenth century), some Venetian authors stated that, in that time, there had been a personal union between Prague and Esztergom in the person of Saint Adalbert. Actually, it is certain that Saint Stephen knew him as a young man, and that the death of Saint Adalbert, the martyrdom of Saint Adalbert, caused a commotion in the court of Géza, in Esztergom. This is why the cathedral, which was built in the early years of Saint Stephen's rule, when he, already as a Christian king, was beginning to organize the hierarchical structure with Esztergom as the metropolitan see, the first cathedral in 1006 was consecrated to Saint Adalbert, who is still the patron saint of the cathedral today.

We also keep a relic of his head, a piece of the skull, which is missing from the whole skull that is kept in Prague, in the Prague cathedral, so therefore [we know it is] from the same person.

Then it was especially the disciples of Saint Adalbert, these Slavic monks, who remained here in Hungary, and the first three archbishops of Esztergom who are known by name come from this Slavic group of monks. So Hungarian Christianity had this resource, but they also had missionaries from Germany; there were Italian missionaries, Saint

Gerard and his group from Venice. Saint Stephen also had family ties with the house of Orseolo of Venice, and after his death, he left no heir, because his son, St. Emerich, had died before his father.

And so Saint Stephen, in order to save Christianity [in the kingdom], wanted to leave the throne to Pietro Orseolo, who became the second Christian king of the country, so all of a sudden they had an Italian. However, the Hungarian traditions called for another system of succession to the throne. It was supposed to pass to the oldest member of the ruling family, which was Samuel Aba, also a Christian, but perhaps less zealous—some accused him of heresy, but it does not seem to have been proven—so it was a Hungarian, who had a claim to the throne, who started a civil war against Orseolo. This war lasted a very long time, with many victims. In the end, both of them died, and a revolution of the pagans began. This revolution was aimed at eliminating the Christian churches that had been built, as well as the priests, especially the bishops, who were still, for the most part, foreigners.

So these pagan insurgents threw several bishops into the Danube from the mountain that is now named after Saint Gerard, among whom Saint Gerard was the most well-known. But these martyrs then became a point of reference for the Christian revival in Hungary.

How was Christianity restored? With the return of a prince of the House of Árpád, who had had to flee abroad during the last years of Saint Stephen's rule and who then had taken up residence in Kiev, and who was connected by marriage to the house of the Princes of Rus. He returned from Kiev with Russian troops and reestablished

Christianity. This was Andrew I, who found the middle
way between Hungarian traditions and the necessary integration into the Western social and cultural context as well.

**So, there are so many centuries, but being Hungarian has
to do with the language and the cultural history, and the
political history. It is not clear where the limits, the boundaries of this are.**

In the Middle Ages, *Hungarus*, or the Hungarian nation, to
Western universities such as Bologna, Paris, meant a subject of the Hungarian crown, so it was a dynastic concept.
Even in the seventeenth century the great Miklós Zrínyi,
who was a great military genius, but also a great writer,
wrote the sentence, "I am Croatian, and therefore Hungarian." Today this would be impossible. Either Croatian
or Hungarian. But at that time, it meant, "I belong to the
Hungarian crown."

So, there were many peoples throughout the Middle
Ages, in the Carpathian Basin, who spoke another language
but who were politically integrated. Croatia had political
autonomy because it was already an organized state when
in the eleventh century the Hungarians occupied Croatia in
order to have access to the sea.

**There are three important topics. One is the topic "Prot-
estantism"; second, the topic "Turkish, Ottoman, and
Islamic," and third, the topic "the Habsburgs, the monarchy" . . .**

All of this refers to the modern era. But the modern era found a Hungary already very rich in colors, in languages, in cultures. For example, the bourgeoisie in all of the cities, even in this city, was German-speaking, exclusively German-speaking. Only in modern-day western Slovakia was there a Slavic-language city, where the city statutes were written in the Czech language, whereas in all other cities they were in German.

Because they were more civilized?

Because the crown needed craftsmen, educated people, people who could work in industry and so on, and they welcomed the Germans with various privileges.

Then, that means in a sense that the Hungarian people had a cultural kinship through this upper class with the German people, with German culture . . .

And especially with the Slavic peoples, who were in the country.

But the Slavs are not Germans . . .

No. Then there was always an orientation toward Italy, especially in the higher classes of society. Everybody studied in Italy; they had marital ties. In the cultural sense, the Italian influence was always strong.

And then this question of Protestantism . . .

It is a later thing. Much later. We are still before the Turks, and now we find before us a country with many languages, with different cultures, but under one crown.

. . . that is Catholic?

Catholic. At that moment, at the end of the fifteenth century, the country was almost exclusively Catholic; the Muslims who had traditionally been present were gone. In the time of Saint Stephen, there still existed these Muslims, because perhaps among the Hungarians or the joined people there were some who were Muslims.

It is said that it was in some ways a golden age around 1480.

Yes, let's say, under King Matthias.

This period of Hungarian history was the golden age?

Yes, it is one of the golden ages.

But then how can you explain the identity under the influence of the Turks from the south, and the Austrians?

Austria was born later. King Matthias, in the 1400s, in the second half of the fifteenth century, still occupied Bohemia, wanted to be king of Bohemia; he occupied Austria, a part of it, certainly Vienna; he wanted to reunite the region a bit, to better withstand the Turks. The bulk of his army consisted of the so-called black army, who were Czech soldiers, fierce, who knew the military technology of the time, but who were in reality, as in Italy, *condottieri*, paid soldiers. This was the system.

Then, among the Hungarian nobility, which was, let us say, the class that upheld the intellectual and military identity of the nation, as well as the political identity, there were quite a few who did not speak Hungarian, who spoke various other languages. And so the country's official language was Latin until 1837. This is a fact.

In this way, one can better understand also how close we are, for example, with the Slovaks. Because it was the same political context in which we lived. We lived together. This diocese, my diocese, bordered directly on the diocese of Krakow for 770 years, and nobody said that it was a Hungarian diocese, but rather that it was a Catholic diocese in Hungary.

When was the time of great innovation and change? Perhaps the Enlightenment, the Napoleonic period?

So, let's return again to the Turks. The defeat at the Battle of Mohács in 1526 was really the end of a chapter in our history. After that, the Ottoman Empire organized itself in the center of the country, so we became an imperial territory. Here in Buda, there was the center of the *Pashalik* with some pashas who were also famous, with some Muslim saints, some churches, many Christian churches were converted into mosques. The authorities generally left a church for all Christians in the cities.

Then the Protestant Reformation began, as bishops could not even come here. And in the north and west of the country where there were no Turks, the episcopal sees, for a long time, remained unfilled because the yearly revenue would then be given over to the king. If the benefice was vacant, the income could be used for military purposes. So the pastoral work remained neglected.

So the pastors, the Protestant preachers, had a greater opportunity to spread their doctrines, and there was a period during the sixteenth century when an absolute majority of the Hungarian population was Protestant, in fact, Lutheran. Then the differences began to arise, especially along ethnic lines, between the German-language Protestants and the Hungarian-language Protestants. The majority of Hungarians then adopted Calvinism. In this way, the famous Hungarian Calvinist Church was born, which was strong especially in the principality of Transylvania, which was a vassal of the Ottoman Empire, but was governed by Hungarian, mostly Protestant princes.

The Counter-Reformation began in the west and north of the country, where the Habsburgs were able to organize [societal] life.

Certainly, the constant wars had as an effect the disappearance of much of the previous population, so that the number of inhabitants in Hungary in 1686, when Buda became once again Christian—or in other words, was freed by the Christians—was only the third of the population prior to the Battle of Mohács. And those that remained were by no means all Hungarians because many Slavs had come from the Balkans, Muslims, like today in Bosnia. They were an important element in various cities. Then many Christians from the Turkish empire came—for example, from Georgia, from Armenia—who worked in business, in small industry.

So, a pluralistic country to the maximum extent, and then . . . ?

And then the Turks evacuated their troops and also part of the civilian population. Of the [civilian] population only a few remained, so the court of Vienna . . .

Why did they evacuate?

Because the Christians were stronger, otherwise they would have been destroyed. For example, in Esztergom, when Sobieski won the victory in Vienna, he continued to pursue the Turks and won also the battle of Párkány, a town next to Esztergom, in modern-day Slovakia, on the Danube. After that victory, the bey of Esztergom negotiated with the Christians and surrendered Esztergom without a fight. He was able to evacuate eleven thousand people.

We are around the year 1700?

1683.

Immediately after the battle of Vienna?

Yes. And it wasn't until three years later that they were able to occupy Buda, because Buda was stronger.

There was almost the risk of the loss of Hungarian identity in these centuries.

The loss of the ethnic Hungarian element at the center of the country, yes. Meanwhile, in the principality of

Transylvania, they began to conduct state life, public life, in Hungarian. So the first state which released its laws in Hungarian was the principality of Transylvania and not the kingdom of Hungary, which always used Latin.

Transylvania was actually a vassal principality of Turkey, but with autonomy. Unlike the center of the country, which was imperial territory, the region east of the mountains, Transylvania, was a principality with a certain autonomy, which had to pay taxes, but which could organize its own life, so it remained a majority Christian area. Some Protestants even came to a common agreement, not on religious freedom entirely, but tolerance.

And then we have the century that led to Napoleon.

Between these, there is still a little bit [of history], because the Hungarians, after liberation, rebelled against Austria. There was the long struggle of Rákóczi, of the Kurucz [anti-Habsburg rebels], from 1708–11. In the end, they were defeated. Prince Rákóczi himself was a Catholic, but he led a resistance that was also composed of Protestants, who were afraid of Vienna, of the Counter-Reformation, which was one of the motives of the rebellion. Then, of course, France supported this uprising because they were enemies of the Habsburgs, but the support was not enough: a few officials who came to train the officers, but it was not enough to resist. So Rákóczi lost and went into exile first in France, then in Turkey, where he died. There was always this nostalgia for the previous ruler, who in the tradition began to be perceived in a more sympathetic light.

But the fact is that under the Habsburgs, they started

to reorganize the country, and they sought especially man-power to re-cultivate the land here, in the center of the country, which had been left almost depopulated. My pre-decessor, Leopold Kolonics, the archbishop of Esztergom, who was even before his appointment as a bishop the only Catholic bishop who remained in Vienna during that battle, during the Turkish siege, drew up a very detailed economic plan for the court of Vienna on the re-cultivation of the most valuable lands. He said, "We lack the population, so we must grant privileges to the peasant communities from the empire, Germans, Slavs, et cetera, preferably Catholic, in order to begin life again." Of course some of his Protes-tant opponents—because he was also a strong figure within the Counter-Reformation, so there were some very harsh differences—but his critics say that he wanted to make the Hungarians poor, Catholic, and slaves, but he never said that. So his project was carried out, and many of the people who now live in Hungary are descendants of those farmers who arrived as part of this project of repopulation.

Meanwhile, the majority adopted the Hungarian lan-guage, but not all. Aside from the Roma ethnic group, which is the largest ethnic group in Hungary, the largest nationality, the largest linguistic nationality is still German. In other words, there is a German-speaking minority in Hungary, which now is not so great because, after the Sec-ond World War, many were driven out. However, in some regions, they remained.

So, the Catholic faithful in this country, who now are still the majority, are for the most part descendants of those Catholics who arrived in the eighteenth century, and they have every right to be Hungarian. They speak Hungarian, they feel Hungarian, and they have contributed a great deal to the development of this country. So if they are not Hungarians, then nobody in America is American.

But are they German, or what are they? Slovak?

They are Hungarian. For the most part, they were German, although there were some from Bohemia—that is, Czechs—then a few from Silesia. The Slovaks were within the country.

And also Croats?

The Croats, yes, several.

Then, this country becomes part of Austria.

No. Part of the Habsburg Empire, never part of Austria. And it was the Jesuits of the Counter-Reformation who developed the legal theory of the *Corpus Juris Ungarici*. This meant that the Kingdom of Hungary was a sovereign state under the rule of the Habsburgs, but it was not a part either of Austria nor the Holy Roman Empire.

But it was a good period, a good thing?

Yes, flourishing. They restored the infrastructure, they built churches, cathedrals.

After Napoleon?

No, before. 1720–1780.

Then what happened?

Then came Joseph II, with his Enlightenment absolutism, who wanted to introduce Enlightenment ideals; however, in a way that was too fast and not organic . . .

But why were all these Enlightenment philosophers born at the end of that century, and after centuries of Catholicism, why did they all become almost enemies of the Church? They wanted change; they thought of the Church as a medieval thing, it was not modern . . .

The Church was at that time the main force which organized the culture, not because someone wanted it to be that way, but because there was no one else. So all of the old educational system of Hungary, prior to Joseph II . . .

Yes, but also elsewhere in Europe . . .

. . . it was based on the religious orders. Jesuits, especially, but then also Piarists and others. Then also the healthcare system. The hospital and things of that nature.

I wanted to say, about the Enlightenment, sometimes it is said that it was the birth of a new kind of Deistic, anti-Catholic Freemasonry, which wanted a Europe that was no longer Christian, no longer Catholic, but Deistic, enlightened. Why did this come into being?

Joseph II did not say that. Ultimately, he characterized himself as a Catholic and he wanted to say what Catholicism meant. He was a critic of the old system from within. That is why Frederick the Great of Prussia would always joke when dealing with Joseph II, saying, "Ah, brother sacristan" because, in fact, Joseph II also prescribed how many candles could be lit during the Mass. He entered into the details. But also, he introduced some good things, reasonable things, regarding agriculture.

The Enlightenment in Hungary was not a result of societal and cultural circumstances, but it came to the country from abroad. Among its main representatives, we find nobles, who were military officials in Vienna for a long time. Similarly, there were Church-men among the enlightened. The enlightened modernism under the reign of Maria Theresa was sympathetic to many Hungarian bishops. The anti-Church methods (banning monastic orders, closing down the seminaries), those came under Joseph II, and later the effects of the French Revolution changed the thinking of the people. Many of those who were earlier sympathetic toward the Enlightenment turned toward the conservative values, but others found the radicalism attractive. This latter point of view was not widespread among the bishops.

I am pursuing this line of questioning in order to arrive at the present day, and we still have two centuries. There is a century in which industrialization occurs; I do not know what role the Church played. Then there is the twentieth century, in which a large part—at the beginning there is the collapse of the Austro-Hungarian Empire, then there

is the arrival of Hitler and the Germans, then there is the arrival of Communism. Now we have the twenty-first century. I would like to understand, but first, we should talk for a moment about these past two centuries in order to then understand the ways in which Hungary can thrive politically, culturally, and religiously today.

So, first of all, Joseph II. He, during the course of the general modernization process, made some errors, which caused a general rejection by society. In his ecclesiastical policies, his religious policies, he had critics, but he also had allies. The Protestants were happy, but when he tried to introduce German as the official language throughout the empire instead of Latin, nationalism skyrocketed. He had opened Pandora's box, because the greatest Enlightenment thinkers in Hungary—such as, for example, Ferenc Kazinczy—were allies of Joseph II to the point that they were even ready to help him introduce the German language, but in order to do this, they first needed to take a survey: how many people, at least among the public employees, among the public administration officials, knew German. Kazinczy was one of the members of the emperor's commission charged with investigating this. The result was less than 20 percent. It was immediately clear that it was impossible. After this, Kazinczy and his friends began working to reform the Hungarian language, to make it capable of being used in modern science and modern science and government.

The first half of the nineteenth century was characterized by a form of conservative absolutism, marked mostly by Metternich. In this time, the Hungarian nobility was able to assemble the parliament many times. They suggested different economic and political reforms. But most of these failed due to the resistance of the court of Vienna, due the fact that the majority of the nobility wanted to keep their privileges, mainly not being taxed, and they resisted the liberation of the serfs. The nineteenth century is the age of the strengthening of both national culture and nationalism. The problems of the minorities living in the country could not be solved in the nineteenth century.

In 1848–49, a revolution and freedom fight broke out against the Habsburgs, which—led by Lajos Kossuth—wanted to achieve radical goals. But the revolution was defeated with Russian help in 1849. Until 1867, Hungary did not have a political government, and its transformation into a unified state in the Habsburg Empire was not successful either. Even though there were experiments to introduce German as an official language, these were met with resistance in Hungary and elsewhere, too. In 1867, the Hungarian ruling class compromised with the court of Vienna. From that time, the country had greater independence within the empire. In Hungarian politics, the former liberal opposition and the Protestant aristocrats became a major force, which influenced the state of the Catholic community in an unfavorable direction.

At the same time, the tension between the minorities grew. There was also a significant economic growth at this time. Even though the liberation of the serfs was carried out, it happened in such a way that in the villages a great number of vulnerable people were left. As a consequence, a mass emigration to America started. The Hungarian bishops organized the pastoral care for the Hungarians in America.

AGAIN, THE SOVIET TIME AND MINDZSENTY

Then, the nineteenth century in union with the Austrians, which ended in the First World War and the Trianon Treaty, in which it was decided to decrease the size of Hungary by two-thirds, to the point that Hungary became a country surrounded by itself. And then, the complicated years between the two wars, the arrival of the German Nazis, and then, the arrival of the Soviets after 1945. Cardinal Mindszenty lived during that period. Can we speak about him and, in speaking about him, try to understand a bit more of this modern history?

Yes. Mindszenty was ordained a bishop right in March of 1944, just days after the German occupation of Hungary. Because of that, the three newly appointed bishops of that time were ordained in the same ceremony here, in the Basilica of Esztergom. Mindszenty occupied the episcopal see of Veszprém. At Veszprém, he protested strongly against the deportation of Jews, against the behavior of the Hungarian Nazi authorities, so the Arrow Cross Party [Hungarian National Socialist Party] arrested him, imprisoned him together with his priests, even with the young Lékai, who was his secretary in Veszprém and who accompanied him in prison. Then he was released after the death of Cardinal Serédi in the spring of 1945. There was a vacant seat for more than six months; then in the fall of 1945, Mindszenty was named archbishop of Esztergom.

And how old was he at that point?

He was fifty-three years old, I think, at that time. Ten years older than Serédi had been. Serédi was particularly young, but he also died young.

And Mindszenty was prepared for this task?

Mindszenty was well-prepared in the pastoral aspects because he had done a wonderful job in the county of Zala, where he had been the parish priest of a city, and then also during the short period in Veszprém, he had shown that he had clear principles, that he was ready to commit himself, to put himself in danger for the sake of the truth, which was his conviction. In this sense, he was definitely prepared. His knowledge of languages, for example, was not so broad. Serédi, on the other hand, had quite an international character.

And Mindszenty had ten years during which there was not a full occupation by the Communists . . .

Mindszenty had three years of effective service in Esztergom, from late 1945 until the end of 1948. In 1948, there was already full Communism in Hungary.

How did he react to this change?

Certainly, he protested when he could, for example, against the nationalization of the schools. Of course, he was unwilling to accept when they requested an act of acceptance on the part of the bishops for the suppression of all religious orders. And the bishops rightly said that they were not qualified to give consent to such a radical step. Only the Holy See is qualified to suppress a religious order, of course.

And the attitude of Pius XII, and of the State Secretariat, did it give support to Mindszenty or not?

The Holy See saw that this was not a unique case but rather a general phenomenon of this entire area, so Pius XII, for example, wrote a moving letter to three archbishops who were in prison at that time: to Wyszynski, Mindszenty, and Stepinac. The latter is now venerated as Blessed in Croatia. All three were in prison because there were these projects with the agenda of destroying the Church and of course arresting the head of the Church, the head of the Catholic community was one of the required steps.

And didn't they almost succeed with this agenda of destroying the Church?

I wouldn't say so. They managed to destroy many things— for example, Catholic schools, even the religious orders— [but] the dioceses survived. The parishes survived even though all such associations had, naturally, been banned. The property of the Church was completely expropriated, even the small parish lands. This forced secularization caused perhaps a bit of resignation and indifference, but it did not have the effect of instilling Marxist belief in the people.

In the vision of the Marxists, of the Communists, it was impossible to let the Church live because it was the opiate

of the people, but perhaps there is a middle way that was being sought . . .

I would make a distinction because, during Stalin's time, Communism was very radical. Later, gradually, they began to talk about coexistence.

Exactly, but was coexistence possible?

We are alive.

And Mindszenty, however, remained as a model of intransigence.

No. Mindszenty was not opposed to coexistence. Mindszenty often spoke out strongly against the injustices of Communism, of that radical Communism, it is true. But intransigence on his part? I don't know. He understood the grave situation of the economy of the country, the poverty of the peasants. Of course, later they introduced the Kolkhoz system and the peasants were not able to keep anything of that land.

Then Mindszenty made the famous choice in 1956 to go to the American embassy.

If it was his choice . . . because today it is documented that he was received in the embassy with the words, "For you, the right to asylum has been granted from Washington." He went into the parliament that morning because, at night, he had been called on the telephone by the Deputy

Prime Minister Zoltán Tildy. And this politician [Tildy] seems to have prepared the asylum of Mindszenty when Mindszenty himself did not know that he had to go to some embassy. So, he was, during those few days of freedom, rather a passive subject of the events, or one that was beginning to understand the actual situation, as he said in his first speech. He did not have the necessary time to develop his own vision or attitude.

But then he became the so-called conscience of the nation, a lone man in an embassy for days, weeks, months, and years.

For fourteen years.

Fourteen years, and he never went out during those years?

What does "go out" mean? Within the diplomatic territory of the United States, perhaps he could stay for a little while somewhere else on the premises, but he did not leave the diplomatic zone of the United States.

How can you judge the attitude, for example, of Paul VI toward him? Can we see it as a tragedy?

I don't think there was such a strong antagonism as some people say between Mindszenty and Paul VI. Both fought for the freedom of the Church. Mindszenty, above all, at the national level, in Hungary, which he knew, and Paul VI globally.

So in this context, Paul VI also should be evaluated because some traditionalists today say that he was weak, he was indecisive, he could not make decisions.

I do not think so. I never saw personally Cardinal Mindszenty in my life, because when I was born, he was already in prison. But I had the privilege of personally meeting Paul VI. Paul VI had an aura, I would say, a charismatic aura of warmth and love. He had an extraordinary personal motivation, enthusiasm for the Hungarian cause, for the Churches here in the Communist countries. It was not just a passive attitude, it was a matter of the heart [for him].

To return one last time to Mindszenty. How is he remembered today in Hungary? As what kind of a figure?

I believe he is a saint. It is not by accident that, as a bishops' conference, we requested his beatification, so we appreciate his spiritual legacy, his memory, his splendid testimony.

CHAPTER 17

THE CHURCH AMONG
OTHER FAITHS

"Christianity can and must look to Judaism, including
in the depth of its theological dimension."

As BISHOP and cardinal, you must lead the Church, but you
must also meet, discuss, talk, and work with non-Cath-
olics, Jews, Muslims, atheists. Europe has many currents
of faith and many currents of agnosticism and atheism. In
France, at the end of the last century, the Church had as a
"leader," in the archbishop of Paris, a converted Jew, Cardinal Lustiger. Were you a friend of Cardinal Lustiger of
Paris?

I respected him a great deal. I almost saw him as a father
figure. He was also the promoter of this circle of [pasto-
ral] missions in large cities. I have him to thank for many
pastoral initiatives which we have been able to achieve in
Budapest. Unfortunately, in 2007, when it was our city's
turn, Lustiger was no longer present, but it was his successor, who has worthily represented the Church of Paris, the
current Cardinal Vingt-Trois.

And what future can we see for relations between Christians and Jews?

I do not know what the future holds, but I know how we must, how we should address this issue. With a great opening, with a radical decision, and with passion about the need for the understanding and rediscovery of our brotherhood, as well as about the need to know each other better, in order to have a deeper self-knowledge.

It is not just about a political opportunity or an intellectual opportunity that exists today, but it is a theological issue that is almost as great, or similar, to that necessity that characterizes the efforts for unity among Christians. That is why, in the Holy See, dialogue with Judaism is not under the dicastery which is responsible for dialogue with other world religions, but under the dicastery which is responsible for ecumenism; although we do not call it ecumenism, in the technical sense of the word, this dialogue nevertheless has a value for us, a special function theologically.

Yes, it is strange that if Judaism disappears, this also damages the cultural context for at least the last two centuries of Christianity, because when the sense of the sacred disappears, the sense of the human being in the image and likeness of God, which are values or ideas brought forward by the Jews, the Jewish community, and the Jewish faith. When the world becomes secularized, when there is no longer any concept of the sacred, when you no longer have an idea of man as the image and likeness of the eternal God, this Christianity itself loses its ability to be present in that society, it also falls toward a secularization. I

think there is cause for an alliance, for a collaboration with believing Jews for these reasons.

And certainly, Christianity can and must look to Judaism, including in the depth of its theological dimension. No other religion has this need. So, the presence of a Christian framework must be, will have to be, and ought to be also useful for the Jewish world.

One more thing, if you'll allow me: as a canonist, I have the personal conviction that it is necessary to have a certain type of modern analysis that is based on individual cases because the great principles of religion and the daily practice are two different things. We have to build a bridge between underlying theological convictions and concrete action of people. Faith is manifested in concrete cases. It is not just an abstract dream.

Historically, culturally, our legal-canonical practice is similar to the practice of the *halachic* tribunals of Judaism, which are relatively rare in the world, but they exist. To solve their cases, they often employ a reasoning which is very similar to that of our tribunals, there are some common basic elements. Saint Paul says, in fact, "Do you not have an intelligent man among you? Why do you bring your litigations or judicial cases before the pagan magistrate?"

So, the ecclesiastical tribunals, the jurisdiction, the judicial activity of the Church is as old as the Church itself, or even older. I think even the method, the way of thinking is a common heritage, which at some moments in history even had interconnections, such as in southern France in the Middle Ages, in Montpellier or in certain works of Abelard.

Abelard wrote a dialogue between the philosopher, the Christian theologian, and rabbi; in other words, this type of environment was something that he was familiar with. Even among the canonists, some were familiar with this method of reasoning. I think we need to seriously re-examine our experience with solving the concrete problems of life, concrete moral problems, and even disciplinary problems of our own community.

Does a Jewish community exist today in Budapest, and there is a rabbi?

There's a Hebrew university, there are twenty-three synagogues, there are three or more different branches. The largest synagogue in all of Europe is here. It is a community that many believe includes about 100,000 souls, although the majority, of course, are not practicing, not religious.

Are there any relationships or work-related ties or friendships with this community?

There are working relations, friendly relations. There are also forums for dialogue; there is also a Judeo-Christian society that organizes conferences and publishes books every year. There are relationships with universities and among the universities. There is also a collaboration in our meetings with the state, where the major churches in the country, or the churches that have the most bearing on the history and cultural identity of Hungary, meet with representatives of the state. The representative of the Jewish community is always there, so we talk amicably before the meeting, and we go together to talk and deal with state officials.

Can one imagine a just peace in Israel, and how important is it to reach this?

Of course, a just peace is very important. Indeed, peace is the work of justice, as is stated in the Old Testament, and as Saint Augustine repeats, "*Opus Justitiae Pax.*" But it is an extremely difficult path. It is difficult when it takes a commitment of all men of goodwill. Just the effort of religious believers is not enough, it takes a more general commitment, and prayer should never be neglected. Even the prayer for the Holy Land, the prayer for peace in Jerusalem and the Holy Land, the prayer for the people who live there.

CHAPTER 18

AFRICA

"Thank God, in Africa, there are many
vocations, including to the priesthood."

Then I also wanted to speak for a moment about Africa.

The Council of European Bishops' Conferences has institutional relations with SECAM, the alliance of Episcopal Conferences of Africa and Madagascar. We have an annual thematic meeting and sometimes even large meetings. In addition to that, I was able to take part in the Synod for Africa, which was a great experience for me.

Because?

Because I heard for weeks and weeks the testimonies, the speeches of the African brothers, and first of all, I was struck by the high theological level of these speeches. I have been present at other synods, synods for the whole Church, and I found that this synod had a theological level that was often higher than the general sessions of the synod. Then I was also struck by the intimate proximity of the European and African cultural roots.

What does this mean?

When we feel the misery of some of these countries—the major problems of society, of the economy, the civil war—then certainly the faithful, but also the local bishops, ask, why is this happening? Have we sinned, or what are the reasons for this? And we Europeans had to ask this as well. What comes to mind is the time when Jesus Christ was asked if the crippled, or those whom the tower of Siloam fell on, or their forebears, had sinned. He said that neither they nor their forebears had sinned but that "unless you repent, you will all likewise perish." So this is a significant message for us as well.

Then on the other hand, this idea of suffering, of being affected because of the sins of the forebears, which we know from the Old Testament, emerged even in the rituals of the Baroque era, especially in the formulas for exorcism in our diocese in 1600, which call for freeing the individual of the negative effects of his or her own faults as well as the faults of his or her ancestors.

We have seen some African brothers say that there are abuses because some priests undertake the healing of the entire family tree. In other words, they pray, they even offer Mass to remove the effects of the sins of the ancestors, which, according to the thinking of many, are the cause of diseases and of the misfortunes of the current generation. So this way of thinking, the problem of witches . . . We are in Europe, and in our cultural history, it is very interesting to see this proximity.

Because in Europe there were . . . ?

Of course, until the nineteenth century, we were full of these ideas, even, at times, superstitions. Christianity, when facing this spiritual world of ideas, must respond. The response is not so fast; the impact of the Christian faith is gradual in the different classes of society. And all this is a common element [shared by Europe and Africa].

Then, of course, there were many other aspects, such as ways we can be in solidarity, or also the question of vocations. Thank God, in Africa, there are many vocations, including to the priesthood. But the great importance that our African brothers have placed upon the education of priests and religious there in their homeland, it is remarkable, even for those who have the intention of later going to serve elsewhere. Because there is a certain culture shock, if a young person comes to Europe, begins to study here, a religious person can lose the context for their life and can end up absorbed by material things. Then they either abandon their vocation or they begin to think of their vocation in more economic terms, or they even leave the novitiate and do not return home, and they are lost.

Or the issue of immigration, with so many aspects. Of course, when there is drought, when there is civil war, when there are threats to life, everyone has the sacrosanct right to try to survive. On the other hand, you can not tell the Europeans that they are obligated to allow the whole world into their countries, because that would break down the public order that is still so attractive to everyone else. In twenty years, there would no longer be any reason for anyone to come to Europe. So we have to find the truth in these situations, to seek a true balance between the key elements of solidarity and mercy.

Then those who come into Western countries, even if they come legally, are subjected in a way to the pressure of not only social integration, because integration is a good thing—in other words, finding your place, figuring out your own appropriate legal status, perhaps entering the workforce, learning the forms of communication of the society. All this is positive. But when there is a pressure to abandon one's own cultural and linguistic identity, this is too much. If one values one's own heritage, he or she must be able to keep it, just as the peoples of Europe are proud of their own languages, their history, and their cultures.

There are two or three phenomena: one is colonialism, the exploitation of primary resources in Africa . . .

. . . which unfortunately continues today. Although there are no longer colonies, the exploitation continues. Not only the earth is exploited for raw materials, but also the people who live there can not sufficiently take advantage of the wealth that the country produces. This problem naturally has different elements, various parties who are responsible, both within the country and abroad.

Many times, it has been said that Europeans have exploited African countries and have, almost as a cover, given missionaries the opportunity to aid in schools and in hospitals, also in churches and in religious instruction, but that in the end, this was not enough. An African once told me it would have been better if you Europeans had never come to Africa.

Certainly, this is a serious conversation. Nowadays, in the globalized world, we have to look at the fact that people move between continents, and that Africa, especially, is a continent that many people want to leave, for reasons that are very understandable from a human point of view. Certainly, all of us say that we should provide help at the place of origin [of these problems], we should ensure that life is possible in their homelands because the vast majority of people want to be happy in their own country, they want to find a job, they want to have a normal existence. The majority of people are not adventurers—even in the case of America, what was the situation? At least from our region, it was the poor who could not find work who emigrated, those who had nothing to eat. They waited for months until they found a place on a ship in order to come to America and to look for work and the possibility of existence there.

Then there is the phenomenon of Islam in North Africa and the rest of Africa below the Sahara, where there were in the past only Christianity and traditional religions, but now also Islam is making inroads from northern Nigeria.

Perhaps in the eastern part of Africa, Islam also has a tradition, further south; that is, on the coast of Zanzibar, Tanzania, in these areas. But it is true that the center of Africa today is a territory where a certain competition among religions exists. I also believe that Christianity in Africa, and Catholicism in Africa, they were never at any point foreign to that continent.

Thanks to God and thanks to the wisdom of the twentieth-century popes, the clergy is, for the most part, indigenous; even the bishops come from the country, with all the difficulties and all the problems that this may entail. For example, if there is a civil war, or there are ethnic conflicts between different tribes, certainly this often affects the clergy as well. But it is that very clergy who can understand the people much better and establish contacts more easily.

It should be remembered that there was a Roman period in which there were figures such as Saint Augustine who lived in Africa. Even if Rome's influence extended only along North Africa's Mediterranean coast, the faith in Africa dates back to the early centuries.

Of course, especially in Ethiopia, there is also a continuity of Christianity since antiquity. In Egypt as well, there is the Coptic Church, which today seems at times to be a victim of violence, which for us is very sad.

We must be in solidarity.

To the extent that right here in Budapest there is a Coptic community. Now they have built their own church. Until now we have given them a Latin Catholic church to use for their liturgy.

So you have given them this church or they are building another church?

They are building another church of their own.

There is the phenomenon of racism, the problems in South Africa, under apartheid, and then the whole process of overcoming this. What can be said about this?

In South Africa, in the general development of the country and the establishment of democracy, there are some aspects that have also been present in the development of Eastern Europe. There were dictatorial or authoritarian regimes that impeded freedom in many respects. Then there was a transition without a revolution, a non-violent change, which was desired by the international community and more or less desired and accepted by the people as well. And we thank God that we also did not have a civil war. But the cost of this peaceful transition was that many problems and burdens of the past have remained unaddressed and continue to produce bitter effects in people's souls. Then they sometimes discredit goodwill initiatives and allow a certain criminalization of these societies.

For the Holy See and the Catholic Church, is Africa a major priority?

It has the greatest importance, of course. Because of the large number of Christians, because of the need for understanding and solidarity, and also because the problems that are manifested in that continent, secretly or not so secretly, are present elsewhere as well.

Are there any African leaders in the Church, or even outside it, who are good friends of yours?

Certainly, I know many African bishops. One of them who I really think highly of is Cardinal Turkson, or from the older generation, certainly Cardinal Arinze and several others. The cardinal who was prefect of the Congregation for Bishops, Bernardin Gantin, had a personal quality that was unforgettable for me. He also visited Esztergom when I was a professor there.

What impression did he make?

To be so intelligent, so sensitive, and so deeply spiritual as Gantin was is extremely rare. I have known very few men of his level who had the courage not to remain in Rome but to return to his homeland when he retired, despite the difficult health circumstances and the lack of comforts in that country.

I have also noticed often in Rome students who arrive with two or three national languages. For example, a Nigerian who can learn Hausa, Yoruba, Ibo . . .

. . . and can speak English of course.

And these are four languages. They arrive in Rome and learn Italian and then study Latin and Greek, Hebrew. Then they spend the summer in Germany or France and they end up having seven, eight, nine languages . . .

During the African Synod, I found among the experts some theologians who were also very well-prepared, some

biblical scholars and other scholars, so it is a young generation that, on average, is very well-prepared.

**And the idea of a pope from Africa . . . ? (Silence) Okay,
okay . . .**

An old law of the College of Cardinals . . .

. . . that one doesn't speak at all about this kind of thing?

While the pope is alive, one should not talk about what his
successor will be like. This is a tradition that dates back to
the Middle Ages. So those that do talk about it are either
unaware of the tradition or trying to be interesting.

CHAPTER 19

LATIN AMERICA

"I'm also very interested in the indigenous pre-Columbian cultures of Latin America."

MAYBE WE can do another continent.

Another continent that perhaps I know a bit better than Africa is Latin America. I have always had a romantic fascination with Latin America because when I was a boy, in high school, I read a lot about Latin America, including the records of the missionaries, the witnesses of the first generations after the conquest. For example, Garcilaso de la Vega writing about the empire of the Incas. He was a descendant of the royal family of the Incas who left his work to us.

And what can we read in it?

In it we can read many things. The infighting in the empire before the arrival of the Spanish, then the behavior of the Spanish, how it is described. Then, of course, there is Bartolomé de las Casas who is fantastic and who preserves the memory of a cruel and sad reality, the disappearance of entire populations. I'm also very interested in the indigenous pre-Columbian cultures of Latin America, of Central and South America.

I read everything I could. In fact, I even dreamed of being a missionary somewhere. Of course, it was an impossible dream because at that time, there were no religious orders and it was legally impossible to go serve in another country, especially outside Europe. But my interest remained. A few years ago, I was able to attend the beginning of the plenary assembly of CELAM at Aparecida as a representative of the European bishops. It made a great impression on me to hear the various opinions, the attitudes of the bishops, and then also the reflections of the bishops about a social reality that is very difficult. In some regions, there is great poverty.

There is also significant economic development in other regions. Then there is obviously a search for justice within the society. There are some phenomena which are similar to problems that we see in our own country. For example, there is neo-paganism, where there is support for certain political trends that want to restore some pagan religion that is no longer fully known, but it was certainly cruel in many ways, and yet is idealized.

In which country?

In various Latin American countries; for example, in the Andean countries.

The Church draws lessons from everything. In Brazil, for example, the Catholic Church has lost many faithful who have gone over to evangelical groups, or even to non-Christian sects. But it has analyzed this experience and it has begun to give a response. So at least now this phenomenon of abandonment of the Catholic Church has slowed. This is important.

The development of Catholic universities and other facilities is also important. The experience of Buenos Aires is a beautiful one; the Catholic university of that city is really a good university. Then I have also seen spiritual movements that were born in Latin America that are also active in this diocese of Budapest. So, the missionary work is not a one-way movement. Now they come from Latin America. For example, there are the Servants of the Poor of the Third World, who come from Peru, or there is the Shalom Community, who were invited by me because I saw in Brazil the good work they are doing. Now they have five members in Budapest. They are learning the Hungarian language with sweat and tears. They know how to dance, they can sing, they know how to play music, and they undertake this kind of evangelization. They already are in contact with groups in our diocese who engage in similar types of ministries. Actually, last year, Cardinal Odilo Scherer of São Paulo came to visit these faithful who are here to do missionary work.

Very beautiful. This phenomenon of liberation theology, how has it turned out in the end?

I think it is no longer as acute as it was decades ago, certainly there [in Latin America]. There were several horizons of understanding because we in the Communist world have known various terminologies that perhaps elsewhere in the world sounded more authentic. But the reality that we saw was not at all attractive, and so we were a bit shocked when others released declarations that were far too positive. Certainly, there were positive things in all countries and there are still. But these praises seemed exaggerated to us.

CHAPTER 20

ASIA

"I am struck by the optimism of the Indian bishops."

WE CAN speak about another continent, Asia.

I must confess that I am not so familiar with the ecclesiastical reality of Asia. I know many Indian priests. For example, a few weeks ago we had a priest from India, a diocesan priest, who came as a *Fidei Donum* priest to our diocese to help in our work. *Fidei Donum* means that a priest is lent, with his consent, by his bishop to another diocese where there is a shortage of clergy.

So priests come from various countries in this way, and now from India. Then there are religious from India in the "Societas Verbi Divini"; the superior of the Hungarian province of the Salesians was a Salesian from India. I ordained four priests a few days ago (2011). Two were from Hungary, one was Italian, and one was Indian. His mother also came to his ordination.

These are two very large countries.

I am struck by the optimism of the Indian bishops. They always say that the Church is about to flourish, that there are many who have an interest and respect for the Catholic

Church, and that many want to convert despite the phenomenon of violence against Christians, often despite the situations of persecution in some Asian countries. I am very optimistic, and my optimism in this respect also extends to China.

And how is this possible?

It's a very large country with a great culture and a large number of Christians as well. Of course, it is such a huge country that there are different legal and social conditions for the Church in different places. With Macao, et cetera. Even Shanghai is different from Beijing.

CHAPTER 21

RUSSIA

"A complex reality, but one that must be respected."

AND THEN we have Russia, which is European in part, Asian in part, and we did not speak about Russia when we spoke about Asia. In these two places, are you familiar with the main figures and the problems, the challenges to remaining hopeful?

Among the Catholic bishops, I know almost everyone. Certainly, the new Archbishop of Moscow, Paolo Pezzi, is a very likable man, which I value a great deal. His predecessor as well, who is now in Belarus, Monsignor Tadeusz Kondrusiewicz, who knows very well the reality of Russia. He has done a great deal to learn, to deepen his knowledge, to propagate the Catholic faith. In Russia much was done to deepen and propagate the Catholic faith and also to raise the level of the Catholic theological education.

Can we consider Russia as a mystery, an enigma, something indecipherable?

No, in my opinion, it is a complex reality, but one that must be respected. In that sense, I also appreciate the efforts of the Orthodox Church, which is now working for the re-Christianization of Russia. The missionary work of the new evangelization in Russia is mainly being done by the Orthodox Church. Culturally speaking, this seems right.

Russia had this tradition of Christian faith. Then there was an attraction in a certain sense to the French Enlightenment.

But where? Among the upper classes of society, not among the common people. There are photos, the tsar after the major feast days, after Easter. On those days, he distributed the kiss of peace by kissing a biscuit, and then touching other biscuits with that biscuit, he gave them to the people. So he did not give the kiss directly but through this other biscuit; through the delivery of this other biscuit, the kiss of the tsar was sent.

Is it in any way possible to imagine that the Soviet period was also a good thing, part of the divine plan? Or was it something entirely diabolical, something negative?

Everything that happens in history can have positive effects. Indeed, in the Easter Proclamation, we sing *felix culpa*, so even sin can have positive effects through God's wisdom. Communism destroyed many millions of men. It was characterised by the hate against the religion. But I would not say that everything was negative. This attempt also contained a certain correct element within it. Large errors are not completely false; they hold some truth.

What is that?

That there is a need for social justice. This was a basic fact, especially where the people were being severely exploited. This need provided the moral justification. Later, this impulse often became merely an ideology, but often it allowed people who came from miserable circumstances to be able to study, to have an honest day's work. So it is not true that it was entirely negative and catastrophic. It had terrible effects, but it also contained something positive that could at times manifest itself.

We are now twenty years after the moment of transition, but prior to that, it appeared that Hungary, Poland, and Russia would continue for centuries under Communism and state atheism. There is something providential in this change that has taken place so rapidly.

We have watched this change unfold almost like a miracle because the transition did not arise from within Hungarian society. We did not struggle to achieve this in '89. The Hungarians fought in '56, but afterward . . .

You were resigned?

Yes, we concluded that the world did not want it. So if the whole world did not want it, we would not succeed, and everybody more or less followed that way of thinking.

The danger is that when we no longer have a vision of things greater than ourselves, whether in a materialistic Communist system that speaks of this world as the only place to find happiness, or in the secularized Western humanistic

world, the consumerist world, there is a loss of memory of things greater than ourselves, and because of this, there is a lack of meaning, there is a lack of beauty . . .

Let's return to the topic of anthropology. We have said that the highest good in life is not simply momentary well-being, feeling good in this moment. For our human dignity, if we wish to experience more happiness on this earth, we must have the knowledge that we are precious, that we are important, the knowledge of values and of rational thought, of the meaning of life; in other words, our place, and the role we play within the context of the universe, in the divine context. In this way, even our happiness on this earth is greater if we do not think only about grain and wine, as the psalm says.

But why is it so difficult to hear these words?

I have heard this from several priests, these types of arguments.

But in general, popular culture seems to be de-Christianized, not merely secularized, but without *logos*, without any feeling of transcendence.

But now, in Europe, many are writing about the Camino, the path of Compostela. Even non-believers have found that this is a special attraction, the path that leads to the sanctuary, to this structure. Today, people are more readily willing to make a long pilgrimage to arrive at the sanctuary than to read a book on religion. That's how it is. So we must also respect this. I said before that we are having the experience of the re-awakening of the sanctuaries and of pilgrimage. The hunger for the holy is still present, even today, but many seek it in other ways and in various forms.

There was a word earlier that I wanted to go back to: God loves. We do not want to be too catastrophic or too negative. The human being in this world is greatly loved. "God loves man." What does this mean?

To love means to desire the good for another person, the true good, not just what he or she desires. Certainly, the two often coincide, but not necessarily. Because God wants our true good, sometimes he does not satisfy our desires, but through heat and cold, he seeks to guide us toward the great encounter with himself. For this, he gives us the ability and gives us the situations, opportunities in life when we can decide for good or discover goodness, and we can express ourselves freely.

CHAPTER 22

LAW AND THE COMMON GOOD

"They cannot be arbitrary. Human beings do not have
the authority to simply promulgate anything we wish
as a juridical norm that all are obligated to follow."

WHAT IS the law? What is the behavior of a citizen in private life? A customary behavior? What might a government overlook when changing or reforming the law? Just as now in the US and Europe, there is a reform of the law on marriage.

I see that you are very Christian, because like the great medieval thinkers, you always speak of the *legge* [statute] and not of *diritto* [law]. It's interesting. Perhaps we can reflect on this point as well.

Yes, there are many points. It seems that today there is a complete absence of wisdom and historical knowledge within the population, which seems to be very plastic. It seems that one can shape, one can create any legal order.

This is the problem because certainly the *diritto* or the *legge giuridica* [juridical law] is a set of norms, a standard that must follow other rules of a higher level. For example, everybody must recognize the laws of nature. A state can not legislate against Newton's laws.

It seems that we want to do this as well, and if we go in this direction, we end up with an irrational contradiction.

But the purpose, the vocation of juridical law, of legal norms, is, in the end, to influence the social behavior of people. So if the law remains unreal, it will not be followed; if it is impossible, no one will follow it. And indeed, no one will be obliged to follow it because *impossibilium est nulla obligatio*, as was said already in Roman law.

We are talking about the law, but not only the law. We are also talking about human lives and organization and justice in our own lives, as well as in the face of great injustices. So the decision is: how do we make a happy life, a good life, a just life? Does the study of the law shed a particular and more precise light upon this issue?

There was a distinction made already in antiquity in the West, in the Greco-Roman world, between the moral level and the legal level of the rules of human behavior, which was perhaps one of the consequences of the crisis of the sophists. Since that time, those who deal with the laws of this world seek a connection between the norms of human society, the norms of external behavior, and the deeper reality of morality; in other words, with the natural *legge*, the natural *diritto*. Some call it *diritto* [legal rights]. Others say that the word *diritto* is too human, its meaning is too connected to a social reality, that we are speaking about another level of reality. However, it is certain that human juridical norms follow a standard. They cannot be arbitrary. Human beings do not have the authority to simply promulgate anything we wish as a juridical norm that all are obligated to follow.

Isn't that exactly what happens in despotic or authoritarian regimes?

In authoritarian regimes, there is an attempt to do this, and here I want to emphasize that in the modern period, Western thought has taken a different step, another step. Whereas before, we distinguished betweem the level of *diritto* (positive law) and that of morality, or *diritto naturale* (natural law), or *diritto divino* (divine law) keeping some kind of connection between them, since the beginning of the modern age this has turned into a separation. If we are atheists, we now either deny the reality of norms of a sacred nature, of a nature superior to other norms that could regulate our legislative and legal activities. If we are deists, then we do not believe in the possibility that the divine level can have some project, some influence on our lives. And so we end up in the Enlightenment age with an idea of unlimited sovereignty of the state, of human society. And with legal positivism, the *diritto* is limited to that which certain organs of the state promulgate in certain forms and enforce by their means of coercion, including ultimately physical constraint.

Isn't this exactly the deeper problem in human behavior that we face in the modern age? That we cannot judge right or wrong, but only legal or illegal?

So, in this drama of atheistic humanism, in the words of Henri de Lubac, this drama of the *diritto*, the prelude to this was the development of German legal thought, which at the end of the nineteenth century and during the first half of the twentieth century was predominantly positivist. In fact, Hans Kelsen developed its pure doctrine of law, which was totally formal, and there were other positivists as well, such as Gustav Radbruch. He was an important philosopher of law in Germany before and during the war, and afterward, he had to participate in the Nuremberg trials and he had to change his position. He changed out of conviction, because, as he said, if we are authorized to do everything that the law of the states allows or prescribes, then we end up with the things that happened in the Third Reich, and this is impossible.

So we must find a way to check ourselves, to keep everything within limits, even human power. Legal positivism is not sufficient for this. There was a certain return to natural law, natural justice in international relations. There was reference made to humanity, to good human sense, to natural justice, natural law. But in recent years, everything seems to have disappeared.

Therefore there is no foundation. If one does not believe that there is a natural law, there is no foundation, because everyone is his or her own natural law; in other words, individualism . . .

I wouldn't say that. Individualism certainly will or could relativize these ideas, because each person perceives the world and the precepts of nature in his or her own way, but nature exists, the universe exists. So, there are natural consequences of behavior on the one hand, and on the other hand, there is also a consensus in society; most people are not stupid. The majority of people have a natural wisdom, and still today there are points where, even in Western society, a broad consensus is possible. For example, that it is a bad thing to kill an innocent person for no reason. If someone enters a school with a machine gun and starts shooting children, everyone says that this is absurd, this must be punished, we must prevent this. As the ancient Romans said, *neminem laedere suum cuique tribuere*. There are general rules of social behavior, which are instinctively recognized by the vast majority of people.

What is the meaning of that Latin phrase?

Neminem laedere, do not harm anyone; *suum cuique tribuere*, give to each his own. If I buy an item and the seller takes the money and does not give me the goods, everyone sees that this is absurd. Nobody wants to be in this situation.

However, we have almost reached the point of believing that power determines whether something is good, that there is no good and evil. If I am able to take it . . .

This is the very thing that physical force cannot determine: what is right and wrong, what is a duty in our conscience and what is not obligatory in our conscience. External force cannot determine this.

So, let us return to the topic: law, human nature, natural law, and the issues of today, whether with the government of Europe and the marriage law, or in the United States, and also the economic problems. Can something be legal but not right? How can we find justice and just laws?

In the history of thought about the so-called *diritto naturale* [natural law]—and we can even call it natural morality, or rules of justice, natural rules of justice in interpersonal relationships, there are so many names that can be used to refer to what has traditionally been called *diritto naturale*—this reality must be one of the rules that guide the work of a lawmaker, the work of those who apply the law, and the work and lives of those who are subject to the law, and who must follow the laws.

As classical moral theology says, we have an obligation to obey the laws, unless the laws are contrary to morality, to divine law, or the laws are impossible—that is, if they ask for something that is not possible—or if they are unjust, and so forth.

Then, of course, the relationship of the law to the rest of reality determines whether it will function. And we see this in our time, especially in the post-Communist world. There is a moral vacuum because they destroyed the traditions during the Marxist era, but now the Marxist system no longer exists, so today there is a large vacuum in societal morality.

Because of this, these societies begin to become

criminalized, because behind the norms of the law of the state, there is no common sense. There is no morality, there is no widely accepted belief about what is right and what is not right. Therefore, to enforce these laws only by physical force is not possible. We cannot have a policeman follow every citizen, and even if that were possible, then who would monitor the police?

The laws of today's world cannot function if they are not supported by a more widespread belief, if there is not a general willingness in society to follow the laws, to obey the content of these norms. In other words, the laws must be supported by the morality of the society. And if this structure is already destroyed in a society, then what do the lawmakers do? They try to protect the laws with other laws, other regulations, and in the end, the law becomes so complicated that you can't follow it even if you want to, even the state authorities don't understand the law and don't know people's rights in certain cases, or what those rights signify.

So, to avoid anarchy and the criminalization of society, we must work seriously to strengthen the ethical and moral base, or the common-sense base, that supports the law. This relationship between law and morality in the modern age, and even in the medieval period, has had several aspects.

For example, there is a famous principle that is found in the gloss of the *Corpus Juris Canonici* where we find the phrase that there are things that are prescribed because they are duties, and others that are duties because they are prescribed. So there is moral recognition of the authority of a legitimate lawmaker to obligate the people to obey, in their actions as well as in their conscience. This was a widely shared attitude among moralists and among the majority of people until the twentieth century. And it was the absurd behavior of some states in the twentieth century that discredited it. And now it is difficult to say that there is a general presumption of the morality and justice of all legal norms of all states.

Even the First World War was still a war in which many participated with the conviction of their conscience, naïvely. Even among the soldiers in the army, there were many with Catholic or Christian convictions, on both sides. We have very moving journals of French and German soldiers, what they wrote, how they thought. It's tragic, it's sad. In this way, the legal authority of the state was gradually discredited. It lost this moral quality in the eyes of the people. Now it has to struggle to regain this authority, which is also a moral authority. This is a very complex and difficult task, but unavoidable. Because if it is not done, what will happen?

Extreme complication does not make the law more effective! In fact, in the end, it does not function at all. Then out of this comes anarchy, corruption, and the society naturally—because there is no society without rules—returns to the archaic regulatory systems that it followed prior to rational legal culture, such as revenge, blood vendettas, things that we can see in organized crime.

They kill, but they do not kill out of anger. They kill because someone has violated some standard of behavior that exists among them, among criminals. So some type of quasi-law, but very archaic and brutal, is reborn in society if the official law begins to become ineffective.

Because of this, it is very important to fight to retain the moral assessment of human behavior, even when there are new inventions, new discoveries in biology, in physics, and even in economic science. We have to assess the behaviors and situations, the new inventions. And that is why I have a great deal of respect for the Holy See, which has several working groups, various dicasteries, various pontifical councils which do extensive research, including conferences, on how to morally assess these new things.

Can you give an example of this?

Yes, the first example is the searing encyclical *Rerum Novarum* of Leo XIII. When new things come into being, one has to give a concrete moral response.

What was the new thing?

It was savage capitalism, the misery of the workers, et cetera. There were the social issues of the late nineteenth century.

Many no longer know because we are not well-educated, that the critique of capitalism derives from the Church itself.

It derives also from others; it also comes from Marx; it comes from many people, but also from the Church, of course. And similar to the way in which Leo XIII began to reflect on the new reality, there are now research centers, there are places of research, research groups in all fields of life. For example, in the field of bioethics, but also in the area of social doctrine, seeking a moral response to new situations. And we must not stop doing this, even if some people make fun of the Church and say we are always moralizing, always worrying about moral questions. But it is a fundamental duty. Because, if we want our convictions to have any influence on our actions, on reality, then we can not abandon, we can not leave aside this difficult moral reflection.

The question of abortion arises, which has been debated for a century now. I believe it was Soviet Russia which validated for the first time in a formal way, as a state, the right to have an abortion without legal issues; that is, legalized. Then we did this throughout the West, while it is contrary to the tradition of Christianity, of the Catholic Church and of Judaism, and I think also of Islam. How can we see if something debated in this way is just or unjust, whether the law undermines people's rights or protects their rights?

As far as Christians are concerned, there are clear passages showing that Christians, unlike the pagans around them, do not accept abortion already in the letters of the Apostolic Fathers. For example, in the letter to Diognetos, or in the letter attributed to Barnabas, this is implicitly understood. The majority of society perhaps thought differently about this, but Christians had this conviction from the beginning.

Another question: what did they think about the human being? From which moment does the human being exist? The central notion was that of *animatio*; that is, when the human fetus receives the soul. For some time, they believed that this was when it began to move. So the moral thinkers of the Middle Ages and the early modern period made a distinction between the abortion of a not yet animate fetus and an already animate fetus. They rejected both types of abortion, but they characterized the second type as more serious: when the fetus was already mature, when it moved, when it had a soul. But now, due to the development of genetics, the development of natural sciences, we know more about the origin of human life, and we know that already in the moment of conception, the entire process of the development of the human being is mapped out and established. So if circumstances permit, it will be not only a human being but a particular human being, the person who has already been conceived. Therefore the moral theology of today says definitively that God creates the human soul for each of us at the moment of conception. That means that between the animate and inanimate fetus we now do not make a distinction, not because of a changed theological attitude, but rather due to a development in biological science.

So reflection can also have these types of consequences. Then again, there are so many other issues today, in bio-ethics, or possible genetic manipulation, that should be considered, should be categorized morally beforehand. Then we naturally will have to ask if there are also people who are convinced to adopt, to follow that logic, at the level of civil society. Certainly, for this, a very broad consensus is needed.

But to return to our question. The Church, before making a value judgment on any human behavior, must enlist the help of qualified lay people, of men of science. The

Magisterium itself, in order to make a concrete declaration, requires the collaboration of all those who are experts in the field. So for this, a scientific team is necessary, when both theologians and the Church itself manifest themselves and express themselves on these issues.

For example, the Hungarian Bishops' Conference, in recent years, has published some very long pastoral letters, up to approximately one hundred pages. First about social issues, about families, and then two others while I had the honor of being president: one on issues of bioethics and the other on the environment. Many academics and researchers worked together to prepare them, primarily Catholics, including the president of the Academy of Sciences. We, of course, asked for the assistance and used the publications of many foreign experts. Certainly, it is important to do this today before arriving at a final text of these documents that responds concretely to the Magisterium of the Church. To also express these ideas in an understandable way that is clear and incisive for the Hungarian public, we needed this help. So the Church, while undertaking this very substantial process of reflection, must act as a community of all the faithful. The role and the vocation of the laity in these areas is particularly clear.

The pastoral constitution *Gaudium et Spes* says that the laity have as a special vocation the transformation of this world according to the Gospel. Then it says that they have this task especially in the fields of politics, science, economics, the arts, et cetera, so in all fields where there is danger, if you will, where the majority of people, or many of the important trends, are not very Catholic. So, to be present, to be familiar with everything that science, that area of life requires, and to formulate a Christian position, is a very noble thing, and this requires broad collaboration. And the more difficult it is, the more necessary it is to reflect morally in order to help the lawmakers.

But now I will go a step further, because now we are seeing in the world also a tendency to want to go beyond this millennia-old legal system, which is based more or less on morality. Because to some it seems possible to disregard the law and morality, and say that, on the one hand, there are a thousand possibilities of manipulation, manipulation through the media, genetic, chemical, direct electronic manipulation, and therefore the human being is exposed to different influences that make him act without the involvement of his personal will.

So these are techniques that are, in the end, less supportive of the concept of human dignity because they do not appeal to freedom, which is something that the law, even while threatening people with penalties and punishments, does. In other words, the law says, "Do this." Or if you do the opposite, you will be punished in such and such a way. So, here freedom is still in play. But if I am looking at advertisements and tomorrow I go to a supermarket and get a laundry powder in a green box, because the previous day I saw the ad a thousand times without thinking about how much it costs, whether it's good or not good, just buying it automatically, this is already a different mechanism. This is how it works now also in politics, within the structures responsible for making laws, this kind of advertising is present as well.

Previously, there was a tacit assumption within what we might call Western democracy that there are political parties, which formulate the beliefs and interests of certain groups, put forth these ideas before the electorate, and try to convince voters using debate and argumentation.

Now, the majority of people are not as susceptible to argumentation, but the parties still debate, now primarily via advertising: someone who knows how to smile well, someone who has a stylish jacket, someone who has a photo-op while they are playing a sport. They use various forms of advertising and marketing. And that means that the election is no longer the result of a choice. It is no longer the result of a logical step or a logical decision, but rather of other factors.

CHAPTER 23

THE ANTHROPOLOGICAL QUESTION

"Jesus Christ brought and represented a new law."

So, THIS is a profound criticism of our democratic system and our lack of human beings of goodwill who have the ability to decide. It is a culture almost without precedent, a culture which is empty, and into this void are coming significant changes in the law, and in thought, to fill the void, which together create an almost unprecedented challenge to man and society. Is this true?

A famous Italian politician of the center-left once told me that he sees the anthropological basis of Western democracy under threat. This is the problem. If the anthropological foundations are still there, there is still debate, there is still the ability to convince people with arguments. If this is not possible, then what are the elections based on?

And this is one of the challenges. The other side of the coin is the possibility of manipulation in many ways, the possibility of technological control, electronic surveillance, and control of all the steps of all people. Some have the idea or the illusion of being able to abandon the system based on legal rights and morality, and use a system without legal

rights, without morals, based on manipulation and electronic surveillance and control.

This seems to be almost a terrible vision . . .

I do not know if it's terrible or not terrible, but it is miserable and impossible because at some point the human
element has to enter in, even if it is only the human element of who is starting the manipulation, who controls it.
Because as we see, the controls are magnificent, but then on
the news, we hear that on even the most heavily monitored
airplane somebody was still able to get on with a bomb,
despite being flagged several times previously. So there are
no flawless systems. Then, who is evaluating the information collected by these electronic means? At the end of the
day, it must be evaluated by humans. Because if it is not a
human being, if it is an electronic apparatus, it can still fail,
it can still be deceived like a human being, but an electronic
apparatus has only programmed criteria [to guide it].

**If I understand correctly, there is a new challenge. The
Western world declares itself to be free and yet still seems
to fall into a type of slavery, whether to the techniques of
advertising and mass manipulation or to electronic surveillance and oversight. The Church now needs to make
a real effort, like Leo XIII in the face of the social changes
of industrialization in Europe in his time. It will be very
difficult and require a great deal of wisdom and humility to
analyze, to make a diagnosis, almost like a doctor, to give
humanity a bit of hope to find the right way, which is the
way to freedom. Is this true?**

Yes. I think that in the past, the so-called degrees of human development, the development of culture, or of civilization, have been in certain part conscious steps that were desired by many people or by many human communities. On the other hand, there were also natural consequences of certain circumstances. So it is not necessary for us to invent and do everything in a new way, because things happen by themselves, and not only in a negative sense. If we want to speak of a new world order, a world order already exists. Of course, it is not ideal, as nothing is in this world. However, there are some bases, there are several aspects that should be appreciated more. For example, international law. Because it is important that states maintain correct behavior with one another and have respect even for the weakest among them. Otherwise, we are in the jungle. Even in human society within a single country, if only might makes right, then we can no longer speak of a state of law.

So international society resembles human society of long ago. But just as within small-scale societies we have seen several steps of development, we can hope that also at the international level the structures of stability, fairness, and respect for the law will be strengthened. Of course, many legal historians say that international law, as we know it today, was born at the beginning of the modern era because in Europe there were several states that were almost equally powerful. If there are not various states of almost equal power, then what possible sanctions can be imposed in international law? This is also an issue. But I do not see these things as all negative. Then, obviously, there are aspects of the economy that today are very international.

So, the question is not whether we have to navigate, the question is how we navigate.

And here we come to the point: there was an attempt made under Marxist socialism, which seems to have had ideals but in the end fell because there was something wrong with this idea of class struggle. We cannot do an extensive analysis. Now there is a comparison with this other element, which is liberal democracy. Twenty years ago, Fukuyama said that this is the end of history, this is the only possible way forward for man.

Under Communism, they also taught in schools that this was the last stage of human development. Communism, no? And where is Communism now?

Jesus Christ brought and represented a new law. Because in Latin Christianity, "lex" meant first of all the Torah, the five books of Moses. And this Latin Christian terminology dates back to the territory of present-day Tunisia, to the province of Africa, the only province in the Roman Empire where the Jewish diaspora was Latin-speaking. So, examining the roots of Latin Christianity, we can find interesting and fascinating things.

The Church of Rome was, until the third century, Greek-speaking. Then with the influence of the African element in the city of Rome, and in the Church of Rome as well, the Latin language prevailed. But they brought with them various already-established forms of religious expression. And they brought with them also Latin translations of some parts of the Bible that were later called "Italian" translations. These translations were not Italian, they were from Africa. There were certainly even some texts of the Old Testament. When Saint Jerome translated the Bible, he was not able to get all of his translations accepted, to have them pass into the daily liturgical usage of the Church. The Church continued to use some more ancient texts. This is also a reminder of that ancient past.

But let us return to the law and the use and meaning of the word *law* in Latin Christianity. There was a biblical meaning, more ancient, taken from Hebrew, which was in reference to the Torah. Then there was a wider meaning: all of the provisions and requirements of the Old Testament. And so "Jesus has freed us from the weight of the law," as Saint Paul says. They interpreted this to mean that the law, in the sense of all these requirements, is no longer obligatory to Christians as a juridical norm, except for substantial moral laws like the Decalogue. The rest of the Old Testament is also sacred, it is worth reading even in the liturgy, and it contains the great events of the history of salvation and prophecies that refer to Jesus Christ, and it also contains elements that prefigure or reveal their fullness in the light of the New Testament, in the light of the work of Jesus Christ.

All of this means that the Christians regarded their community as a sacred community that also had its own discipline, as well as its doctrine, and this discipline dated back to the apostles and, in the end, to Jesus Christ. And this discipline was regarded to be as sacred as doctrine or the liturgy.

A secularism that would result in the denial of transcendence seems somewhat old-fashioned because today we see many signs of uncertainty about where the limit is when we speak of immanence and transcendence. What is on this side? What is beyond? Where is the line?

I see among the intellectuals a deep uncertainty in this regard, more than a dogmatic reduction of all reality to the level of the immanent, of what is tangible and sensible, denying the existence of anything transcendent or eternal. Immanent with respect to what? Because before, the claim commonly made by materialism was that which we cannot see, that which we cannot touch, does not exist. But that was just the popular understanding. Already Lenin knew that this is not enough to define matter. He referred to matter as "all what exists regardless of our conscience."

But this is good, now we are on familiar ground. Because in this sense, matter no longer has any limit. The most important thing, then, is to seek perfection, as Aristotle did. So you can put forth the question of God even without the category of matter. Because the line between transcendent and immanent does not seem so clear, and that's why many are open, many have an interest in any religious movement, even in these ancient Asian religions or modern spiritual movements. People have a lot of interest. But there is also great uncertainty. Where is the boundary between this world and beyond this world? Our knowledge of astronomy, or physics [can provide answers], but perhaps even these methods also must be put into perspective, in the sense that we have to be humble and know that these sciences provide wonderful and new data, which may also have an impact on our view of the world, but we do not discover all aspects of reality with them. So the immense space for a personal God, a God that we say is transcendent with respect to the entire universe, not only remains, it always reopens in a new way.

How can you try to explain this to a person today, an intellectual or even an ordinary person? What does it mean?

First of all, both ordinary people and intellectuals recognize that we humans do not know the totality of everything that exists. This already is humility. It may be the beginning of a deeper way of thinking. *Initium sapientiae est timor Domini.*

"The beginning of wisdom is the fear of the Lord."

Exactly. So, if we begin with this open attitude, the question of the meaning and value of all the reality that we find around us, of which we ourselves are also a part, will inevitably arise.

Perhaps only revelation can guide us.

So, what does the First Vatican Council say? It says that, already in this world, based on the light of the human intellect, the existence of God, his eternal power and his divine qualities, can be recognized, and it makes reference to the New Testament. But this is not a compulsory awareness or recognition. In other words, it is not like a physical experience, on the one hand. On the other hand, it is not a full knowledge. Full knowledge, which we as human beings are unable to reach, but which came to us in the person of Jesus Christ. God, through a man, has communicated to us all that he wished to communicate, and all that humanity can accept or receive. And so the historical process between Jesus Christ and our time is of paramount importance for us. There is the tradition, the Church, and the testimony of all generations.

So an individual in need of meaning for his life feels that there is a meaning and evaluates or encounters this, either through the teaching of the Church, or through the models of life around his or her community, or through scientific research, or through reading philosophical works. Then comes a moment when he wants to say, "I have found it," like the woman in the house looking for the lost coin, or as in "I have found meaning, the *logos*." The people who give meaning to my life, to my story. That moment is the conversion in which the individual dedicates himself. And within that, there is a dual attitude in a certain sense. There is the joy of giving oneself to the thing that has been found, which seems more precious than anything else, but still there remains the former person, who does not want to take this commitment on his shoulders, and he wants to go on living day-to-day life without any great responsibility, because it can sometimes be heavy, it can sometimes bring persecution. Doesn't it seem that this is very much present in the world today, this dialectic between "yes" and "no"?

Thomas Aquinas wrote in his unforgettable hymn, which is sung so many times in today's Church, *expertus potest credere quid sit Jesum diligere*, "whoever has had the experience can truly believe what it means to truly love Jesus Christ." The encounter with God—and this is a general, anthropological and also theological observation—this encounter is always fascinating and awe-inspiring: *"fascinosum et tremendum."*

We see it also in the Old Testament: whoever encounters God is astounded that he or she has lived to tell about it. So there is fear. Even Jesus Christ, after his resurrection, always begins the encounters with the disciples with "Do not be afraid," because the first feeling is fear, and therefore there is fear and there is fascination. And we must not forget this fascination.

Because whoever has encountered Jesus Christ, whoever has encountered the true God, has the experience of this fascination. This helps, then, also in changing their own lives. In other words, it is not a mere speculation, it is not just a human theory, a philosophy according to which we should try to live more reasonably, but a love, a fascination, the fascination of a colossal being.

This reality is so much greater than us, that already this fact, when we encounter and come face-to-face with it, must transform us. He is the giant above the universe, but also in the world, in history, and in our lives.

It is said that there are no words, there is only silence. Almost like Job, "I heard of him with words from mouths, but now I see with my own eyes and I repent in ashes, in silence, I will say nothing more." Because it is colossal, it goes beyond. Is this the meaning?

Yes.

So you are speaking about a mystical experience, like Jesus, like Moses.

We can judge this experience that is present in every generation, that is had by true people of faith, as mystical. This experience is the true guarantee of the permanence of the faith in the world and the permanence of humanity. Because if we lose engagement with our Creator, we can no longer exist.

All the natural efforts of humanity that have been made in search of God, in search of the true nature of this world, in search of our vocation, deserve respect. This is also what the Second Vatican Council teaches regarding religions. We must not speak of them only as diabolical manifestations. This type of description appears often in Christian antiquity when the nascent Church was surrounded by paganism and various rather cruel phenomena of different religions, but it is also found in the description of so-called natural religions. Certainly, the fullness of the knowledge of God came in Jesus Christ, so he is the center of history, he is the place of encounter with God, and therefore, with all due respect, we are convinced that we have something to say to everyone, to all humanity.

CHAPTER 24

THE GOOD NEWS AS IF FOR THE FIRST TIME

"We have around us, even in Europe, many people who have never known the Christian faith."

THE NEW evangelization: what does it mean, why it is necessary, and how can we carry it out?

Evangelization, the proclamation of the Good News of Christ, is the fundamental mission of the Church at all times, in all ages, and on all continents.

However, in the Western world, after secularization, after the loss of faith by many, the loss of many Christian elements in the culture, it is necessary also to change methods. Pastoral work is not enough. We are faced not just with more or less practicing Catholics; instead, we have around us, even in Europe, many people who have never known the Christian faith. This is the point.

These are conditions for missionary work, for the first proclamation. And this requires other methods, other commitments. It was John Paul II who encouraged the Church to undertake a new evangelization, beginning with Europe. The word has taken on a special significance after the collapse of the Communist world because there were so many things, so many missionary activities that were previously prohibited. So we could take it up again, we could begin to proclaim the Good News in state-run universities, sometimes even in Russia, or in schools, or in the media, or in workplaces. Even the hospitals were no longer forbidden to us. There was the possibility of accompanying even prisoners who had been incarcerated, or soldiers, all the areas that had previously been banned. And above all, the masses who were hungry and thirsty for an essential truth about the world, the human being, the purpose of our life, and the meaning of our lives.

Of course, many other new ideologies and many other religions came as well. However, many people wanted to know the religion of their ancestors, the religion that is manifested in churches and monuments visible across Europe, and in this way, starting from a thousand points, missionary work began.

In our diocese, for example, we started the first mission at the parish level. There were mission crosses bearing the dates of each of the holy missions, which ended in the late '40s. And now we see numbers like 2003, 2004, 2005, and so on. Of course, we didn't start this work again using the old method, but we saw the week of the parish that was done in Rome, which was a good initiative. As a first step, we tried to deepen the conviction and zeal of parish workers: priests, deacons, religious, and laypeople who were involved in the parish. Then, as a second step, we had a very detailed liturgical study for the whole parish community. And the third moment was always the step toward the world, in many senses of the word, as well as in a geographical sense.

There were priests who came from the third world, from distant continents, religious who were studying with us or who were in the convent who recounted the experience of their church, or even Hungarian missionaries who had spent decades in distant countries like New Guinea, et cetera.

And then opening to the world in the social sense, in the theological sense: in our own region, we were trying to get in touch, even through the local media, with non-believers who were not familiar with the Church. Then there were even missions in the streets in some regions, even among prostitutes or the homeless, all of this still within the context of the parish mission.

Then there was the mission to the city of Budapest, which was part of a movement comprising five major European cities, and our delegation of sixty people, including priests, lay people, and collaborators took part in the mission to Vienna, Paris, Lisbon, and Brussels. They gained a lot of experience while also contributing to the missionary work in those cities.

Then as a second step, we had a great liturgical celebration for the whole parish community. We involved all of the parishes. There was a week of missionary congress in Saint Stephen's Basilica, and there were many testimonials. For example, the president of the Academy of Sciences testified, and the wife of the President of the Republic (Ferenc Mádl), who had recently passed away and who was a practicing Catholic. And there were also many of our non-Catholic Christian brethren, there was the Metropolitan Archbishop Michael of Austria and Hungary, from the Ecumenical Patriarchate, and others. There were presentations by people engaged in social work, for example, who took care of orphans, or of homeless people, desperate people. There was also a parallel program in various parishes. Then there was the Christian art week. In fourteen state museums, there were thematic exhibitions. There was a Gospel concert on the roof of a shopping center, which I attended and spoke at. I saw that half of the young people were believers, and the other half did not understand any of this.

So, this is the typical situation of the new mission, believers and non-believers who encounter one another in the context of a movement animated by religion.

Then we had processions of the Sacrament in the streets. We had days of penance in different churches, where we offered confession. We had several lectures and round-tables with the archbishops and cardinals of these other cities. We had programs on television, theater pieces in public squares, many things. We published, for example, the Gospel of Saint Mark in the form of a newspaper, things like that. So many initiatives, of which quite a few have remained and are repeated every year because people like them. For example, praying around the city, a 150- or 200-kilometer circuit around the city of Budapest. Various parts of this long road are covered by different groups of the faithful while praying a part of the Rosary, and at the end of the day, they meet in the Marian shrine of Máriaremete. There we end with a Holy Mass and a prayer for the city and the surrounding area. So, there are so many things that have been repeated, and they represent a space of encounter with the world, with non-believers.

There seem to be so many initiatives. But what is the over-arching theme? What is the message that you can proclaim to attract modern people to an eternal thing? How can you present the Gospel in a new way?

"Be not afraid." This is the theme, because many in our world are afraid of the Gospel; they are afraid of Jesus Christ because they feel that it is a demanding reality. But this demand is a demand that arises naturally because of the nature of human happiness. If we want to be truly happy, we must not be afraid of the Good News of Jesus Christ, who is the only one who is able to make us fully happy. So according to our experience, this is the thing that reaches people whom we know to be unbelievers, who watch all of our programs with great attention, and who in fact later come over to us.

I will tell the story of an older criminal lawyer who taught at our Catholic university. We were able to speak only a few times because he was in the Law Faculty and I was the rector of the university, but I heard his lectures at various conferences. Once he asked me—this man, who was a criminal lawyer, very well-known, who had had his experience in the Communist era—"Peter, tell me a bit about the concept of original sin." Dealing with sin in the field of criminal law reminded him of his education in his youth, and he thought of this category of original sin. And because he knew French very well, I found in Rome a book on this topic, in French, and I brought it back and gave it to him. So after a time, he had returned, for a moment, to this idea. Providence works in truly unexpected ways.

Among the modern European and Hungarian authors, are there any authors that are especially profound?

Yes, I love literature. I love the ancient classics.

Why?

Because they are beautiful, they are wise. I read with pleasure the classic authors like Seneca and Cicero. But I really love the modern era, especially the early modern era, the great Spanish authors like Lope de Vega, as well as others, playwrights like Calderon. I also love Russian literature.

Ah, really?

Certainly.

Just like Rowan Williams, the Anglican Archbishop of Canterbury. He loves Dostoyevsky.

Of course. Dostoyevsky is dramatic, he has seen the depths of the human condition, and he describes them with colors that are at times very dark, sometimes, for me, too dark. I also love Tolstoy. There are various other modern authors whom I like, some whom I read in school. To read Mayakovsky in the original is beautiful. I have also been struck by certain novels. There are certain writers who, for a thousand reasons, are close to my heart, like Franz Werfel: of course, "The Song of Bernadette," and many other things. Then also authors such as the American Nobel laureate Isaac Bashevis Singer, whom I think is among the greats because the problems in his greatest novels are theological problems. He not only dramatizes the problems, like many writers, but he seeks and finds an answer that, many times, is convincing and worthy of being shared. So it ends up as a modern novel, very action-packed and lively, at the core of which is, for example, a question like how God can be omnipotent and merciful and wise at the same time. He doesn't talk much about this, but the question is present throughout the novel. There are several like this. In Hungarian literature, of course, there is a Catholic current. I love very much, for example, Mihály Babits, who is a great poet of the twentieth century, or Miklós Radnóti, who was Catholic, but who was killed at the end of the war due to his Jewish ancestry. Then Sándor Sík, a Piarist Provincial Superior who was also a poet. Also, István Vas, who was more of a literary theorist and critic, but who also had some wonderful pieces. I know some people from the literary world personally. I do not say that I love all of the works of any author uncritically. There are of course some reservations even when one speaks of one's favorite writers. But, for example, Solzhenitsyn, to me anyway, is one of the greatest figures of the twentieth century.

CHAPTER 25

POPE FRANCIS

"It was a providential gift to the Church."

POPE BENEDICT, on February 11, surprised the world with the decision to end his papal ministry and live a life "hidden from the world" in a convent in the Vatican gardens. When this news was announced, what did you think?

I thought about what canon law says, that the office of the Roman pontiff is an office whose holder may renounce it, and the renunciation goes into effect immediately, without needing to be accepted by any other authority. This is due to the nature of the office of the pope because he has no superior in the Church.

And then came the moment of the conclave. Can you reflect a moment on what happens during the congregations before entering the conclave? What is the mood that the cardinal electors feel when they come together? Are there any anecdotes that you can tell without breaking the secrecy of the conclave?

Among the cardinals, there is an atmosphere of brotherhood, of sympathy and mutual understanding. Certainly, not everyone knows everyone equally because if one works very far geographically from another, they will have fewer opportunities to meet. However, on certain occasions, we see each other. Then also we hear the opinion, the style of the other. So the atmosphere of the congregations preceding the conclave was, I think, constructive and friendly.

The structure of these meetings closely resembles that of the Synod of Bishops, even in terms of the surroundings, because the meetings are held in the Synod Hall. We have to ask to speak, and when someone has the floor, he has a few minutes to express himself, to make an observation. So almost everyone has a chance to say something. Of course, there might be discussion of the different needs of the Church, different necessities that the Petrine ministry has the vocation to resolve or to help with. Some might also speak about the particular situations of various local churches or certain regions, or about spiritual and theological values. There was a great deal of media interest. In the first days of these meetings, there was no rule that we couldn't talk about the contents of the discussions; it was only after a certain date [that we couldn't talk about them]. This is why the colleagues from the United States, for example, also organized several specially designated press conferences to address details of the discussions. On previous occasions, all of the participants had to maintain secrecy or discretion about the content of the discussions from the very beginning of these congregations.

Two days later, a new pope was elected: Francis, Cardinal Jorge Mario Bergoglio. Can you comment on your first thoughts about this man, and about the prospects that

opened for the Church at the moment of the election and the first meeting of the new pope with the public on the evening of March 13, 2013?

Certainly. A pope who comes from Latin America. For a long time, there had been talk about the importance of this continent for the entire Church and for humanity, and also about the particular experiences of the Latin American Church that seemed to be enriching for the universal Church. It was evident in his first words, and even in how he greeted the people, that the personal style of the then-Cardinal Bergoglio was also fascinating. The fact that some were expecting an Italian, and then there appeared a man who is Italian, but who belongs to Latin America, whose identity is Latin American—and Catholic, which is far more important than the rest. The Catholic Church truly has a thousand faces across many cultures and continents, many pastoral situations. So it is a type of enrichment, and many hoped, and many still see now in the person of the Holy Father a larger opening in practice toward the universal aspect of the church. At the same time, the choice of the name Francis immediately had a special message of immediacy, simplicity, openness to the poor, as the Holy Father says, to the periphery.

After the election, when I returned home, at our bishops' conference, we spoke about the style of the Holy Father and we took note of the fact that we, as the Hungarian Church, as a country in Central-Eastern Europe, feel completely that we are on the periphery of the Western world as well, similarly to Latin America during its history. So, there are also feelings of closeness and similarity in the situation of these two large regions.

Then there was the invitation to the pope to visit Hungary . . .

This was much later, when the president of the Republic, the prime minister, and the episcopal conference all invited the Holy Father to come in the year 2016. This is a year of particular importance because it is the year of Saint Martin of Tours, who was born in Pannonia. This year will be the seventeen-hundredth anniversary of his birth. Saint Martin of Tours was the first saint of the Church who was not a martyr; he was a confessor. So he is a symbol of a new era after the long period of persecution in the late Roman Empire when one could be a Christian. However, he is also a symbol of the moral challenges that accompany this change, because Saint Martin is also the great social saint who helped the poor throughout his life and who cut his cloak in half to give half of it to a beggar. He was a bishop who did not take on the lifestyle of the Roman aristocracy of the time, the kind of opulent lifestyle that other bishops of the time were leading. He provoked a bit of uneasiness because he was not just any ordinary bishop, but one who remained faithful to the genuinely Christian ideal, who did not want to simply give in to the change of circumstances in this regard. At the same time, he was also a symbol of the relations between the Church that followed the genuine orthodoxy of Nicaea and Christians within the faith who were problematic. He intervened at the imperial court, not to defend heresies, but to mitigate the legal actions of the state against people who were considered heretics. So the way in which he dealt with this phenomenon was also very special, deeply Christian. He did not accept without criticism the fact that, from then on, it would be the state that would set and enforce the content of the faith. Saint Martin of Tours is also a symbol of the universality of the Church, of the brotherhood of peoples. In many European countries, he has a very large, very extensive cult. Many, many churches throughout Europe are dedicated to him. The French see him as one of their own saints, and he was also active in northern Italy. In that time, from Hungary to the Atlantic Ocean, there was a single country with a single population that could understand one another, with an exchange of culture, faith, belief, and lifestyle, which becomes very relevant once again today. So Saint Martin is truly a cause for celebration and for inviting the Holy Father, who accepted and welcomed the invitation. But we cannot know for sure whether he can come. With this invitation, it is certainly necessary to specify the details, and now we know that 2016 is also the year of the World Youth Day in Poland. When in 1991, after the fall of the Iron Curtain, John Paul II was able to come for the first time to Hungary, this trip was also connected with a trip to Poland, to the same region. Also, Hungary, from Rome, is not such a distant country, in an hour and a half by plane you arrive in Budapest. It's the same as if you were to visit the most distant city in Italy itself. So it is not far, neither spiritually nor physically.

Then the first months of his pontificate. There were so many surprises, so many unforgettable moments, from the first meeting of the "two popes" on March 23, to the decision to stay in the Domus Santa Marta, to the three "shock" interviews (one on the airplane on July 28, one with the Jesuit Spadaro in August, and one with the Italian journalist Scalfari in September 2013). Can you comment on these first few months? What did they mean for the Catholic Church?

They meant a great deal for the Church. A great deal of joy, many encounters, many messages sent through human gestures, through personal relationships. So we are grateful to Providence for giving us this new pope, and we also see with great admiration how he has resolved an issue that, in the beginning, no one could imagine: how the emeritus pope would also live in the Vatican. But there appears to be a beautiful harmony, and it seems that this is a good, possible model. Certainly, diocesan bishops who have had the experience of a retired, emeritus predecessor also have many positive things to say about this. For my part, I also have the joy of having a predecessor who is a wise and kind person, who lives in the city of Esztergom.

As for the interviews, if one reads or listens to the words of the pope carefully and with a minimum of attention to what the Catholic faith says on these issues, then you feel a joy, a voice that is genuinely Catholic and very modern at the same time. But if one is not familiar with the faith of the Church and hears the interviews from a third-hand source, from a summary of another summary translated into a third language, then one can think various things, but that is the age we live in. Even the manifestations of the Church, of the popes, of the Holy See, the messages reach the people and the faithful very often through the mass media and are filtered through the understanding of journalists who make a summary and who highlight specific things. This is why the responsibility of Catholic journalists is so great and so crucial. They must have an especially profound cultural foundation in order to understand exactly what is being said so that they can convey the true meaning of words and events. It is a very demanding vocation. We talked about this a little while ago in the Congregation for Catholic Education. The university courses in journalism and media are very important things for the Church of today, and it is not enough for a Catholic journalist just to know his profession, but in addition, he or she must have a profound cultural foundation and a very noble human and Christian attitude.

From the beginning, the Church has oscillated between, or has been nourished by, two poles—charism and institution; that is, the Holy Spirit who inspires us when and where it wills, and then all the apparatus of canonical law and hierarchical structure. These two poles may be in tension, or in creative harmony. Now, with the desire of the current Pope Francis for a "poor" and "merciful" Church, some argue that the structure of the Church may be somewhat overlooked, that there is a risk that the hierarchical Church of so many centuries may become merely a movement, that canon law may be less appreciated because it is seen as an impediment to authentic Christian life instead of as an aid. **How can you as a canonist explain the risks and benefits of this situation, of this tension, this "Francis effect" which at the same time fascinates and worries many Catholics?**

First of all, this opposition between charism and institution is artificial. It does not correctly express the theological reality of the Church. Even the so-called institution is charismatic. In other words, the substance of the Church is, according to the Catholic faith, the mystery of salvation and the visible organization, at the same time. The Church is the communion of grace and the visible community. This is how it can participate in the function that began through the Incarnation of the Word of God. This is the teaching of Vatican II, *Lumen Gentium*. So even the so-called institution, the mission of the apostles, the College of Bishops, also the Petrine ministry, the ordained ministers—the priests but also the diaconate—all this and also the sacraments, which are institutions because they are visible, socially perceptible forms that have a system of conditions, of effects, of visible celebration: all of this is a result of the work of the Holy Spirit. When Jesus Christ sends the apostles, the Holy Spirit communicates to them: receive the Holy Spirit and proclaim. The missionary mandate is also a mandate deeply rooted in the Spirit, so throughout the history of the Church, the charisms that we call special, extraordinary charisms, when they are really useful for the life of the Church, when they are strong and effective, when they respond to the needs of a historic moment, they call for institutionalization and are institutionalized, like the charism of Saint Francis. In the beginning, he certainly did not want to found an order, but the Church had so much need of the charism of Saint Francis that it would not let this charism, this divine grace, escape with the death of the saint. It wanted this charism to remain, and so the institution was created. This is what happens in all the histories of the religious orders. In all of the ecclesial movements today, we see the same thing: the institutionalization in modern form of certain charisms. Then, among the charisms, there are some who have a special vocation to judge the authenticity of the other charisms. This is the charism of the apostles, of the bishops. So even the hierarchical function is charismatic. Because of this, I see rather a type of relationship, dialectical, in the noble sense of the word, between the visible institutional aspect and the spiritual charismatic aspect within the Church, never an opposition. At the same time, there is a special charism that arises out of an institutional mission that has the vocation of discernment of the charisms, as we see in Saint Paul.

In light of all this, every revival presupposes the existence of a socially visible reality, and if it is really innovative and profound, it also has an effect on the life of the visible, structured, and institutional community. The Second Vatican Council was truly a great moment of the Holy Spirit within the Church, and yet the ecumenical council is a very institutional thing: it has a precise order, members, modes of expression, and also official documents of different types, constitutions, decrees, declarations. The ecumenical council has its specific authority. Divine grace, the Holy Spirit, is moving in all of this because the Lord God became incarnate and entered into full solidarity with mankind. So, following the Incarnation, we must be faithful to the great example of Jesus.

The Russian President, Vladimir Putin, made a visit to Rome on November 25, 2013. How do you interpret this visit, its significance, and any possible future developments?

In history, the possibilities are infinite. Certainly, it is important that even in countries that have gone through a long period of Communist dictatorship, Christian heritage is being appreciated and the values of the faith are also being considered. Russia, like other countries in Eastern Europe, has had the experience of a moral and cultural vacuum after the collapse of Communism, which had an official ideology of Marxism-Leninism, after which the cultural and moral vacuum brought society to the verge of almost total criminalization. Because of this, in order to maintain peace in society and to establish a more human way of living together, a system of values was desperately needed. The cultural heritage of the nations that lived in these lands was also needed, and what did they find after the massive destruction of the Communist era? Traces of their Christian heritage. It was necessary to reawaken, to revive these values, both in public opinion and in the material legacy: reconstructing the destroyed churches and monasteries, reestablishing the institutions, resuming the teaching of theology and other sciences related to religion. It's no coincidence that with the help of the Russian state they are publishing a huge series, the "Pravoslavnaja encyclopedia" that so far contains more than thirty large volumes, and they are not even to the middle of the alphabet. This is entirely accessible on the internet and is updated several times a month, and it contains many scientific items, many details of religious-cultural history and of the Christian theology of that immense land and also of the neighboring peoples of the Caucasus, Eastern Europe, the Balkans. So, it's something that is very valuable and certainly is a contribution to the restoration, to the re-awakening of an entire culture, about five minutes before those values would have been wiped out. So there are encouraging phenomena, there are values to be respected, there are also risks, as there are anywhere in the world, the phenomena of various crises and transitions, and the search for a way to ensure peace in society and coexistence in some orderly and organized manner in a such a large country.

Are there any concrete collaborations?

First of all, there are diplomatic relations. There is the nunciature in Moscow and there are also diplomatic relations with other post-Soviet republics.

How can Putin's visit help to promote this collaboration?

It can be a concrete expression of goodwill. Certainly, there are many common values to present to the world. It is also clear that dialogue, which is not a matter of the state but is between the Orthodox and Catholic Churches, is in progress, and there are many fields to be explored further. It is certain that we can continue our collaboration within these fields, at the level of social and moral questions: the social doctrine of the Catholic Church but also of the Russian

Orthodox Church, about which we have found several valuable documents. Then there is the European Catholic-Orthodox Forum, which now has hosted three important meetings with all of the European Orthodox Churches. The next time, we will meet in Belarus (held between 2-6 June 2014). We will have many things to deal with. There are acts of reconciliation, for example, between the Russian Orthodox Church and the Polish Bishops' Conference, which was a beautiful document of reconciliation.

As for the study of other theological issues, surely there are prospects still open. From the Catholic side, the request of Saint John Paul II to examine other possible ways of exercising the jurisdictional primacy of the Roman pontiff is very much a current topic. In history, we know of various ways in which this primacy operated. Even today within the Catholic communion, the operation of this primacy of jurisdiction takes various different forms, because in the Eastern Catholic Churches there are many things that are under the jurisdiction of these Churches' own authorities rather than under the Roman Curia. While in the Latin Church many decisions are depending on the Roman Curia, the Eastern Catholic Patriarchal Churches can make the same decisions on their own. This inner independence can have many other forms within the Catholic communion. With the notion of Churches *sui iuris*, is a model, a form of communion that is very fraternal but very respectful of the heritage of each of these Churches. Certainly, in the case of the Orthodox Churches, there are some open possibilities of finding communion and also respecting the dignity that is found within the life and discipline of each of these Churches.

Can the fact that Pope Francis prefers to call himself the bishop of Rome, rather than mentioning that he is pope, help promote dialogue with the Orthodox Churches?

He is still the Roman pontiff, the successor of Saint Peter, and the head of the College of Bishops.

But can it be interpreted as a step toward these Churches?

This is also true. Within the Catholic Church as well, of course. The Petrine ministry is connected with the diocese of Rome, with the Church of this city. This means that even the College of Cardinals is not a parliament elected by the whole Church, but still symbolically represents the Roman clergy, where the cardinals receive their titular churches. So it is clear that the Church of Rome has a special vocation and that the office of the Roman pontiff is a truly episcopal office. This is why in recent decades it was strongly emphasized that the pope ought to be a consecrated bishop, and why many people were concerned, at a theological level, about what might happen if someone who had not yet been consecrated a bishop were elected. "*Statim ordinetur episcopus*" [Immediately let him be ordained a bishop] is what the rules of the conclave say. Because theologically speaking, the entire function of the pope is an especially episcopal, apostolic function, and within this context, it has its own special quality.

Pope Francis has spoken about wanting to "reform" the central government of the Church—the Vatican, the Holy See, the Curia. What are the possible benefits and dangers

of such a reform? Can the Church risk being less united if decisions are made country by country? Or is there a greater risk of an "authoritarian centralism" that represses the authentic local expression of faith?

I think these models of centralization and decentralization are too sociological. In the Church, the model of communion is what is important. This is something that is profoundly organic and has always been so. It can find different forms of expression, of course, but from experience we know that many bishops' conferences are in need of the support of the Holy See and feel much weaker in their own country, whether in dealing with civil authorities or in dealing with society as a whole, without the concrete and direct support of the Holy See. For this reason, we greatly appreciate the ministry of the papal diplomatic corps, which is truly an aid to the local churches. The nuncios have a double function: on the one hand, they strengthen the communion with the local bishops, with the local Church, and on the other, they have a diplomatic mission to the governments of their respective countries. We consider this a valuable ministry, and we are grateful to the Holy See for the support and the help that it gives. Obviously, there are issues that require some local expertise, but today there are so many things that are decided at the local level, and not always even at the level of the local bishops' conference, also at the diocesan level. This is also the theological mission of the diocesan bishops, which is full and fundamental, because the rank of the hierarchy based on "divine right", as the canonical and theological authors stated it. It is enough to refer to the fact that the Second Vatican Council puts such a big emphasis on the role of the bishops. The bishops' conference is one possibility of expression of the bishops' collegiality. Its fundamental task is the joint meeting. It has right of disposal only in the matters in which it is entitled either by the law of the Church or the supreme authority of the Church. Practically speaking, it depends on the universal legislation of the Church, how much is assigned to the episcopal conferences and how much is not. So we can say that the fundamental level of communion and of local Church government is the diocese. Because of this, we need to see concretely what authority can be exercised at the local level. In previous years, there have been experiences with this, for example, with regard to the form of the distribution of Holy Communion to the faithful; in other words, administering the sacrament also in the hand. It was an issue that the episcopal conferences had to decide, and then the Holy See had to give permission to introduce this form as ordinary form. But surely this was not a novelty even in the Latin Church, to say nothing of the Eastern Churches. Already Pope Benedict XIV, in the eighteenth century, expressed permission for communion to be given in the hand to the faithful in times of epidemics in order to avoid infection. The patristic texts are often also mentioned when we speak of the dignity and the form of communion.

You have been appointed Relator General of the synod on the family, which meets in October 2014. Has the pope given you some indication about the path to follow? The dangers to be avoided, the issues to be clarified? Have you talked to him?

The Holy Father received the group in charge of the synod, in which I was also present. The pope gave general indications. And if later on there are concrete issues that materialize during this stage of the preparation, then we will personally turn to the Holy Father with great joy to request more encouragement and advice.

Do you have a vision for the family that can be summarized in a few words, a vision that can be a synthesis to help all participants understand the importance and purpose of this Synod that is about to begin?

The family is part of the fullness of human anthropology. God wanted the family, and the family has a special place in the plan of the Creator himself because the human being does not reproduce only at the biological level, but there are human values that are transmitted from person to person, from community to community. This community can live and gather together primarily in the form of a family. So the community of love, care, mutual help, whatever parents can give to their children: not only life but love, which accompanies the human person from childhood so we can grow and have trust toward others. Whoever does not have this in childhood must be a very remarkable person if they are able to nevertheless learn these rich forms of expression and communication with others and not be hostile or suspicious toward others. The family is a large school where we learn to live together in a human way, so our appreciation for the family is immense. We also say that the family, in some way, is the image of the Divine Trinity. The human being has a vocation to communion, not just to living side by side. All great achievements of human culture are based in a community and have a community character. For example, language, which also influences the development of human beings and communities, as well as the development of human thought itself. The great anthropological changes of the present day necessitate the experience of the family and require the family; they do not render it superfluous. So we are looking forward to the synod with great hope and great joy; we are looking forward to the encouragement of the Holy Father and to encountering so many positive experiences throughout the Church because we have to strengthen one another.

Can you comment on the experience of being in a period of Church history when there are two "popes," one Francis, the other the emeritus pope, Benedict XVI? What does this mean for the doctrine of the primacy of Peter? How can we evaluate this period, from the resignation of Benedict up until the present? Does it create a precedent? In the future, will it be almost normal for a pope to renounce the Petrine office at the age of eighty-five years, or eighty years? Is this idea of a service that lasts until death definitively buried as a tradition of the distant past, or can we imagine that this time now is unique, and we will never again in the future have more than one pope at the same time?

Even today we have a single pontiff, Pope Francis. Pope Benedict is the emeritus pope, as in every diocese where there is a diocesan bishop and there are one or two retired, or emeritus, bishops. On the other hand, certainly, as I said earlier, the specificity of the office of the Roman pontiff is that there is no other higher authority in the Church that can accept or reject the resignation. So if the pope is able to act, if he has control of his capacities, he can freely decide whether to step down or not. If he resigns, this goes into effect without needing any further approval or acceptance. This was always known as a theoretical possibility within the Church, so it is not that shocking for us. As for the future, no one can guess what will happen. Now various articles are coming out that say that Pope Benedict after the resignation, with his way of living in the Vatican, with his prayer, with the offering of his whole life to the universal Church, continues to carry the spiritual responsibility that is connected with the Petrine office, but certainly, speaking of the office in the full sense, since the resignation came into force, he is not the pope. So, there is this spiritual aspect, and there is an aspect that is not only institutional, but institutional and charismatic at the same time, that is connected with the office of the pope, and this cannot be multiplied.

What should we see as the overarching theme of Benedict's pontificate, concluded in February 2013?

It was a providential gift to the Church. Pope Benedict is a great teacher of the faith, both as a theologian at the personal level and as a pontiff who instructed the Church. Also, a man of great sacrifice, who bore many burdens during his service. A man who always had immense pastoral charity and who was already widely respected before being elected pope. One who has done much for the life of the Church and whose teaching will prove to be fertile and profitable in the future. It is interesting and beautiful how the teachings of the various popes of our time connect. One builds upon the other. There is an organic continuity in these teachings, which is a gift to the Church.

What is the overarching theme of Francis's pontificate so far? What is radical in comparison with previous popes?

I do not know whether these categories of radicalism or non-radicalism are relevant. Surely the element of joy is central to his pontificate, both in his personal behavior and in his teaching. The joy of the Gospel. Certainly, the Christian message is a positive message that is joyful, as the arrival of the Savior is a joy to mankind. Jesus Christ brings joy, not sadness. Even the internal spiritual motivation of missionary work, which is the vocation of the Church and of all Christians, is joy; that is, to share the joy that lives in us because of Jesus Christ. This is the central task, and this stands out in Pope Francis's pontificate.

CHAPTER 26

BOOKS: FROM WORDS
TO THE *LOGOS* . . .

"God bless you, and I wish you the very best."

TODAY SOME packages containing books arrive here in Budapest. These new books, which arrived today, what are they about?

Let's see, two volumes of the five-volume series of the *Corpus Juris Civilis* with the medieval ordinary gloss, in the Hugo Porta Lyon edition, which was published (and reprinted) between 1552 and 1558, which is, as they state in the preface of the first volume, the first time that they had printed this monumental work in large format (in large folio) with Roman characters; that is, no longer with Gothic characters, as they did in the late Middle Ages and in the early part of the 1500s. So this was an effort that was also combined with a certain humanistic criticism of the text, with the participation of Hotomanus and other humanist jurists.

When we speak of these things, these books, these *incunabula*, I am impressed by the memory that you have for names, not only of the authors, but of the editors, of the year printed. Is this something that you are truly passionate about, or do you also have a photographic memory?

Not only that. Sometimes, during my student years, I was surprised because I would read a chapter of the study guide at the entrance of the examination room and afterward I was able to repeat the entire text from memory. I myself was impressed by this. But this is just short-term memory.

As for books, I have told about how all my father's books were burned because the house where we lived in '56 was destroyed. So it is important for me to appreciate books.

Your father was very sad to have lost the books?

Yes, also because of this.

It made an impression?

Yes, because he was a lawyer. He also had scientific interests. He had no chance of working in this profession, so he was particularly attached to these books, these documents that he had at home, that he lost because of that fire.

But you were four and a half years old in 1956, or a bit younger . . . at the time of the fire.

Yes, but afterward I also heard the stories of my father about the books that he had once had. And so we begin to appreciate culture a little more, and when we witness the destruction of a part of it, we appreciate what remains elsewhere, and we try to rebuild and start over. Life is like that, no?

Would you describe yourself as a lover of books, of manuscripts? Do you have a passion for this?

Yes, that is true.

Which manuscript comes to mind as particularly astonishing?

There are many splendid manuscripts. During my studies, I worked in the Vatican Apostolic Library, so I used many of the manuscripts. But very near to here there is one manuscript, a parchment fragment which I found in Esztergom in the binding of a book. It is four sheets, beautifully handwritten in the Bolognese style, from around the mid-1300s, and it contains a portion of the *Lectura* of the cardinal of Ostia, Enrico da Segusio, who comments on the Decretals [papal letters] of Gregory IX. This was one of the most exacting works in the science of canon law of that era which was bought by some student in that time and taken home to Hungary.

Can you reflect on one last thing, a passage of Scripture that speaks in a special spiritual way to one who is leaving on a journey, like me, a piece of writing that I should learn and reflect on?

I have in mind the invitation of God to Abraham, that he must leave his land, his home, the land of his ancestors, and go to the land that God will show to him in the future. That is, leave behind human certainty and trust in God to fulfill the divine plan, which even to him is not yet fully known. There's a departure which expresses an act of faith, an act of trust in God.

And why does this sentence come to mind for me?

Because each departure requires trust because we are going to a place where other tasks are awaiting us, where the plan of God awaits us, which we must follow even at the cost of not knowing where we are going. Your work is of great responsibility: as a journalist, you always have to face new situations.

Thank you. I am very glad that I came here to Budapest.

Thank you for your questions, for your willingness to come here. Now you must go. Once again, God bless you, and I wish you the very best.

APPENDIX

Péter Erdő

THE ROLE OF RELIGION AND THE CHURCHES IN A SECULAR STATE

*Lecture at Columbia University,
New York City, January 29, 2018*

LADIES AND Gentlemen,

It is a great honor and pleasure for me to hold a lecture here at Columbia University on a religious subject. I have to confess, I was somewhat embarrassed when Professor Somerville invited me. Choosing the exact theme of this speech proved to be a special challenge. Since my area of expertise is canon law, I had to be extremely careful not to burden the audience with specialist details. So I came up with the topic about which I am going to speak this evening.

Church and religion in the secular state seems to be a present-day question because we are facing a profound, grave crisis which may be summed up in the word *relativism*. This means that we, as a society, are increasingly unable to say something is "right" or "wrong," "true" or "false" (even our news, which is often "fake news"[3]) because, as we say, and generally now believe, it is all "relative."

---

[3]   Pope Francis, *Message of Pope Francis for the 52nd World Day of Social Communications*, 24 January 2018, https://w2.vatican.va/

The Problem

Until the Age of the Enlightenment, Society Was Regulated by a Unified Normative System

As the larger communities of human society form into states, the ultimately physically enforceable rules of social behavior and even the development of the laws themselves claimed that the contents of the law and the authority of the legislators are founded upon factors higher than just the human community. Law, morals, and religion prove to form an organic whole, which is characteristic of Western society right up to the age of the Enlightenment.

The Great Lawgivers From Hammurabi and Justinian Until the Modern Age Placed the Human Community Within the Cosmos, and They Legitimized Both the Lawgiver and the Laws Through Religion

The great legislative works, such as the Code of Hammurabi or, much later, the *Codex Justinianus* begin by situating the particular community into the context of the universe and supernatural forces; that is, they see their place both within the cosmos and beyond it. In the preface to his code, Hammurabi refers to his mission given by the gods,[4] and Justinian begins his work with a confession of the belief in the Holy Trinity.

---

content/francesco/en/messages/communications/documents/papa-francesco_20180124_messaggio-comunicazioni-sociali.html.

[4]   *The Code of Hammurabi King of Babilon about 2250 B. C.*, ed. Robert Francis Harper, Chicago: The University of Chicago Press – London: Luzac and Company, 1904, p. 3.

In the area of the religious and therefore the moral legitimization of state authority, Christianity introduced a special novelty. It distinguished state power *(potestas)* from the authority *(auctoritas)* of the Church. Its classical interpretation is very notable in the letter of Pope Gelasius I, which he addressed to Emperor Anastasius in 494 AD.[5] Here the dualistic principle of Church and State was formulated. In this context caesaropapism, whereby Caesar claimed for himself also the highest Church authority, could appear. On the other hand, from the side of the papacy, there was an attempt, according to which in certain cases—on the basis of Church authority—the pope could extend his authority over the state power, such as in the time of Pope Innocent III or Boniface VIII.[6] Almost in response to this, some tendencies in Western thinking appeared, which claimed that the power of the civil ruler or of the people originate directly from God. In this way, they try to establish a moral legitimization of the civil law, independent from the Church.

In the late Middle Ages, even theological thinkers, such as Gregory of Rimini, came up with the idea that the concept of moral sin can have a basis without any reference to

---

[5] *"Famuli vestrae pietatis"* JK 632.; Heinrich Denzinger – Peter Hühnermann, *Enchiridion symbolorum definitionum et declarationum dee rebus fidei et morum. Edizione bilingue,* Bologna: EDB 1996, nr. 347; D.96 c.10: *Corpus Iuris Canonici,* ed. Aemilius Friedberg, Lipsiae: Bernhard Tauchnitz, 1879-1881 (repr. Graz: Akademieverlag, 1955), vol. I, col. 340.

[6] Cf. Péter Erdő, *Il peccato e il delitto – La relazione tra due concetti fondamentali alla luce del diritto canonico,* Milano: Giuffrè, 2014, pp. 70-73.

religion or God.[7] Later, Hugo Grotius said that natural law would be valid even if we supposed that God does not exist, or does not care about humankind.[8]

Legitimization Comes Not From the Church, but From Wholeness of Objective Reality

In the age of the Enlightenment, great intellectuals referred to a natural law, which can be recognized by the human mind from the world, and upon which laws can be based independently from any religious view. The first declarations of human rights either explicitly or tacitly reflect this philosophical conception. The thought of religious

---

[7]   Gregorius Ariminensis, *Lectura super Primum et Secundum Sententiarum*, Super Secundum Dist. 34-37, quaest. 1, art. 2: edd. Damasus A. Trapp – Venicio Marcolino, vol. VI, Berlin–New York: Walter De Gruyter, 1980, p. 235, 11-24 (*"quicquid est contra rectam rationem est contra aeternam legem, ac per hoc secundum Augustinum recte dicatur peccatum esse factum vel dictum vel concupitum aliquid contra rectam rationem, id est, ut post patebit, facere vel dicere vel concupiscere, quae omnia sub vocabulo 'agendi' comprehenduntur, contra rectam rationem. Si quaeratur cur potius dico absolute 'contra rectam rationem', quam contracte 'contra rationem divinam', respondeo: Ne putetur peccatum esse praecise contra rationem divinam et non contra quamlibet rectam rationem de eodem; aut aestimetur aliquid esse peccatum, non quia est contra rationem divinam inquantum est recta, sed quia est contra eam inquantum est divina. Nam si per impossibile ratio divina sive deus ipse non esset, aut ratio illa esset errans, adhuc, si quis ageret contra rectam rationem angelicam vel humanam aut aliam aliquam si qua esset, peccaret"*).

[8]   Hugo Grotius, *De iure belli ac pacis libri tres*, Amstelaedami: Ioannes Blaev, 1651, (fol. 5r), Prolegomena (*"Et haec quidem quae iam diximus, locum aliquem haberet etiamsi daremus, quod sine summo scelere dari nequit, non esse Deum, aut non curari ab eo negotia humana"*); cf. Erdő, *Il peccato e il delitto* p. 53.

tolerance appears and becomes widespread in this context, since the functioning of the state and the legitimization of the legal system does not depend anymore on the teachings of any religion. As long as the functioning of the state was closely tied to the official religion, the lawgiver himself justified the punishment of certain acts—such as blasphemy—with such reasoning that if they were to tolerate these, God would punish the whole nation with natural disasters.[9] This means that—contrary to the modern concept when certain blasphemous manifestations are punishable because of the sensitivity of other people—in former times, not the societal, but the religious consequences dominated in these cases. The Prussian *Landrecht*, issued in 1794, provided the first basis for this modern, non-religious concept of blasphemy.[10]

During the Nineteenth Century, the Idea of Separating the Law and the State From the Rest of Reality Arises. The Relationship Between Religion and the State Becomes a Problem.

According to the Enlightenment theories, the essence of the natural law was still quite close to the Judeo-Christian moral concept. In the nineteenth century, the philosophical foundations of this concept of natural law start to lose their convincing power. The idea of

---

[9]   Nov. 77. 1.1. Cf. *Corpus Iuris Hungarici*, Budae: Typis Regiae Universitatis, 1779, vol. I, p. 506, art. 42 anni 1563; cf. vol. II, pp. 17 and 166, art. 42 anni 1659, art. 110 anni 1723.

[10]   *Preußisches Landrecht,* Teil II, Sechster Abschnitt § 217, cf. Rusztem Vámbéry, *Istenkáromlás,* in: *Magyar Jogi Lexikon,* ed. Dezső Márkus, vol. IV, Budapest: Pallas, 1903, pp. 387-388.

relativity and the unknowability of the natural law, or the rules of upright human behavior based on its connexion with nature, gains ground, as also does the separation of law from so-called natural morals. Because of this, the *relationship between* religion, the Church, and even one's worldview and the state becomes a problem. This is the question which many experts try to clarify even today. Nowadays, the possibility of an even more radical position turned up, which we will discuss later.

THE QUESTIONS OF THE TWENTIETH CENTURY

Legal Positivism and the Pure Theory of Law

Gustav Radbruch and the Relativism of the Current Positive Law

Moral relativism and uncertainty about the knowability of the natural law led to a point when the trend of legal positivism became widespread among lawyers. Even John Austin states that the existence of the law is one thing, its worth or worthlessness is another.[11] In the twentieth century, strong versions of legal positivism appeared, which considered law as a closed system of positive theses, the content of which is established by given procedures in the relevant organizations of the state. Behind this concept is a certain late version of the Enlightenment idea of the social contract, which does not consider this tacit agreement as a form of legal contract.[12]

---

[11]   John Austin, *The Province of Jurisprudence determined*, London: Weidenfeld and Nicolson, 1955, pp. 184-185.

[12]   Cf. Jan M. Broekman, *Rechsphilosophie*, in: *Historisches Wörterbuch der Philosophie* edd. Joachim Ritter – Karlfried Gründer, vol. VIII, Basel:

For example, Gustav Radbruch was a prominent representative of legal relativism and legal positivism. He went beyond the neo-Kantian principle which held that the law depends on moral values. And, since according to him these are not absolute, then law and justice are relative too. The law, rendered independent from the broader reality of morals, led to horrible abuses in Nazi Germany. The trials of Nuremberg showed where the separation of law and morals can lead. It was not easy to convict people whose actions were based on current, but immoral laws. Later, this contradiction was resolved by Gustav Radbruch himself with the following formula: morals are a basic element of law, and if a law breaks this, then it no longer meets the criteria of legality and therefore does not become applicable. Through this, Radbruch clearly had come to revise his own earlier concept and depicted law as a system open to the world of ethics.

The Hart-Devlin Debate

In the Anglo-Saxon world after the Second World War, the Hart-Devlin debate had great repercussions, where the main question was whether the law is a completely closed system, or by various mechanisms needs to be connected to morals in the seamless fabric of society and not artificially cut up into separated sectors. Naturally, the correlation of law and morals never meant, and never can mean, that everything which contradicts morals should be banned or punished by the law. Regarding this, even Seneca has

Schwabe & Co., 1992, pp. 320-321.

provided a very pragmatic theory in his *De clementia*—his essay addressed to Emperor Nero.[13] Here he stated that those sins, and even crimes, which are very common cannot be severely punished.

Is the Legal System Functional on Its Own, Detached From Other Social Norms?

But this did not resolve the problem which arose from the uncertainty surrounding natural morals, and from doubts about the knowability and contents of morals. Would it be possible to say that we can legally enforce morals if we cannot even establish what the content of morals is? In this matter, different anthropological views became apparent. The questions became: who is the human being? What is the good of the human being? Is the existence of the individual human being, as well as society, a part of a great project, or should it be, or indeed can it be, up to the human person himself to determine?

On the other hand, the difficulty turned up that the positive rights of the state are not really functional if the voluntary, law-abiding behavior of the citizens does not back it up. You cannot put a policeman next to every citizen, and then, even if this were possible: *quis custodiat custodes?* Who guards the man on guard?

Problems of the Socialist Legal Systems

Precisely because of these questions, many worked on the problems of socialist morals in the former Communist

---

13   *De Clement.*, I, XXII, 1.

countries. The aim was to promote voluntary obedience to the law. But since, within the framework of Marxism-Leninism, there was no form of religious legitimization, nor, in a broader sense, any form of recognition of natural law, a great number of conferences and studies came up with the result that the content of socialist morals is always the current Penal Code. But if the content of morals is simply the Penal Code, then this kind of morals will barely be able to strengthen the authority of the laws. Former French president Nicholas Sarkozy encountered the same problem and propounded in his book *The Republic, Religions and Hope* in 2004 that it is not sufficient to educate youth based only on the esteem of the values of the state and the Republic. He considered it good to reduce the space between the state and the religions, and to integrate religious communities much more into society. The basis of this thought was the realization that the state is in need of a kind of moral support to function properly, and also needs values which itself is unable to create. It needs to draw them from society and also from religious communities. It needs to rely on the values they offer.

An "Expedient Law" or a "Just Law"?

After the epistemological turn of the second half of the twentieth century, many started to doubt the existence of objective goods and tried to narrow the question down to the problem of desires and interests based on a subjective choice. That is how they reached the more relative and formal concept of justice and its separation from the common good, which they declare to be unknowable, or even non-existent. So the majority of the modern theories of justice have a more political character and are detached from the traditional legal outlook. Many consider as a principle that what is expedient is prior to what is good. "They consider the latter, subjective, because in society there are many concepts of good, whereas justice, which is seen to be a complete whole of the rules and institutions which make coexistence possible with respect to the liberty and equality of its many subjects" is objective.[14] Another question is whether societal coexistence itself, which maintains the liberty and equality of subjects as an aim of the law, does not itself imply some kind of objective good?

According to authors such as John Rawls "that logical justification, which is needed by some metaphysics, morals" or even "some Churches and religions, refer only to those who accept them, so it cannot be part of the organizing principles of the State."[15] But this point of view is not accepted by those who are in need of truth and believe that they have to turn to everybody, "not only to those, who share their views."[16] Even if certain branches of state power deny the existence of knowable goods, even they, tacitly have to accept certain requirements of co-existence in order to influence the behavior of society. In Western societies, there exists a certain layer of "civil honesty," which—despite the ideological differences—enables the functioning of many institutions.

---

[14]   Giorgio Del Vecchio - Francesco Viola, *Giustizia*, in *Enciclopedia filo-sofica*, Milano: Bompiani, 2006, vol. V, p. 4885.

[15]   Del Vecchio – Viola p. 4885; cf. John Rawls, *A Theory of Justice*, Cambridge (Mass.), 1971.

[16]   Del Vecchio – Viola p. 4885.

Lessons From the Fall of Communism

Ideological Vacuum and the Danger of the Criminalization of Society

There is a different situation in the post-Communist world, especially in the former Soviet countries. In these regions, the bourgeoisie was always weak, and Communism destroyed the economic structures as well as the structure of society. Religions and morals were supposed to be replaced by the Marxist-Leninist ideology. After the fall of the regime, a cultural and moral vacuum was born, which endangered the functioning of law and state, and also led to the danger of the criminalization of society. It is understandable, therefore, that in certain countries, politicians are not too attracted by relativist ideologies. Instead of this, they are busy trying to rebuild the cultural and religious foundations of their society. A minimal consensus in certain (objective) values is a cultural prerequisite of democracy. These values cannot be merely formal but have to suppose some elements of the common good. Furthermore, Western democracies suppose from their very beginning that people are able to recognize the common good and elect those institutions of the state which are meant to guarantee it.

The Need of Ideological and Moral Foundations

The State Cannot Create These, They Have to Be Drawn From Society

As we have already mentioned, for the functioning of the law, we need certain ideological and moral foundations, which can be widely accepted. It has also been proven historically that, other than by using force, the state is unable to create these. It is worth looking at the former Communist countries again.

Religion and Churches as Factors of Value

After the fall of the Berlin Wall, the laws on the freedom of religion and conscience were reintroduced one after another in Central and Eastern Europe. In many countries, new constitutions were accepted. In these laws, Churches and religious communities are mentioned several times as factors of importance and of value in society. For example, in Hungary in the preamble of the fourth law of 1990, it was explicitly said that "churches, denominations and religious communities in Hungary are entities of prominent importance, capable of creating values and communities."[17]

The preamble of the agreement of 2000 between Latvia and the Holy See recognizes, among others, the contributions of the Catholic Church to the religious and moral development, societal rehabilitation, and re-integration of the Republic of Latvia.[18] The preamble of the concordat between the Apostolic See and the Slovak Republic in 2000 recognized the role of the Catholic Church in the social, moral, and cultural field, and also reflects on the Cyril-Methodian spiritual heritage.[19] The moral

---

[17]   Balázs Schanda (ed.), *Legistaltion on Church–State Relations in Hungary,* Budapest: Ministry of Cultural Heritage, 2002, p.43.

[18]   Cf. *Enchiridon dei Concordati – due secoli di storia dei rapporti Chiesa–Stato,* Bologna: EDB, 2003, pp. 2190-2192.

[19]   Cf. ibid. p. 2213.

contribution, along with the Cyril-Methodian heritage, which is basically Christianity itself, has a prominent value from the point of view of the Slovak state. We could list a great number of examples from the laws and international agreements of the former Communist countries. From the formerly capitalist countries, it was Greece which stated in its constitution that the ruling denomination in Greece is the Eastern Orthodox Church.[20] But these basic agreements do not describe the way in which the state counts on cooperation with the Church.

The claim of cooperation, however, turns up in other countries; for example, in Articles VII, XV, and XVI of the Hungarian Basic Law.[21]

Religious Freedom as an Individual Right, and the Special Legal Treatment of the Churches Which Are Prominent in the Culture of a Given Nation and Religion, as an Identifying Factor

In many countries of Europe, the question of individual religious freedom and the special place of religions in the identity of a nation often arises. The latter is a social fact, which the states themselves wish to take into consideration. One of its clearest manifestations was the communiqué of the Second European Catholic-Orthodox Forum in Rhodes in 2010. In this, the bishops' conferences of Europe, the Vatican, and practically all European Orthodox Churches pointed out that in European countries, the

---

[20]   http://www.hri.org/docs/syntagma/artcl25.html#A3.

[21]   Balázs Schanda, *Religion and Law in Hungary*, Alphen aan den Rijn: Wolters Kluwer, 2015, p. 23.

recognition of religious freedom as an individual human right is growing. It is contained in the European Convention of Human Rights of 1950 as well as in the Charter of Fundamental Human Rights of the European Union in Nice in the year 2000, as also in the constitutions of many countries.[22] At the same time, they refer to article 17 of the Lisbon Treaty, which considers Churches as subjects of the national legislation, and also recognizes their unique contribution to the identity of Europe.[23] This fact provides the basis for the legislation of the member states, which has the right to treat certain religions and religious communities as a specific category. The Catholic and Orthodox Churches intend to participate actively in the ethical and moral debates, which influence the future of society. They are convinced that European countries cannot omit their Christian roots without the danger of their own destruction because these ethical norms are the key to the future in a globalized world.[24] The same thought is expressed in the communiqué of the Czech, Slovak, Croatian, Polish, and Hungarian bishops published on October 19, 2017: "We pray and work . . . for a Europe which respects the individual and collective religious freedom which belongs to the human person by virtue of his own dignity; for a Europe which also recognises the possibility of people to respect in a just manner those religions which have contributed

---

[22]   Catholic-Orthodox Forum Rhodes 2010, *Communiqué*, in: Consilium Conferentiarum Episcoporum Europae, *Church and State relations: from Historical and Theological Perspectives, Atti del II Forum Europeo Cattolico Ortodosso*, Bologna: EDB, 2011, pp. 216-217.

[23]   Ibid. p. 217.

[24]   Ibid. p. 218.

in a major way to the formation of their own culture and identity."[25]

Behind these statements is the recognition that Churches and religions in practice and in reality contribute to the creation and maintaining of the system of values and moral foundations of society. As mentioned, there are some rules of civil honesty not attached to a particular worldview, but they are, nonetheless, relatively widely accepted and followed in the Western world. However, in the former Communist countries, these rules function much less.

In his dialogue with Jürgen Habermas, Cardinal Joseph Ratzinger mentioned that the two great cultures of the West—that is, the Christian faith and the culture of secularized rationality—do have a role in shaping the whole world and all cultures, but they do not have always a real influence. The former Communist world, especially the former Soviet regions, are good examples of where the borders of this universality lie. On the other hand, the fact that in these countries the political class often sees Christian values as important for the functioning of society might indicate that the Christian worldview is more widespread and lasting in these regions than civic thinking with its own economic prerequisites and philosophical tendencies. The story of an old Benedictine priest is very characteristic. He spent many years in the Soviet Union, in the Gulag work camps. At the beginning of the 2000s and coming close to his one-hundredth birthday, he joyfully said, "I was

---

[25]   http://www.ccee.eu/news/news-2017/307-19-10-2017-europe-must-be-a-true-family-of-peoples.

dragged off to be destroyed because of my Christianity. But I am still here, and where is the Soviet Union?"

Contradictions in the Idea of "Hostile Separation"

The theory of the separation of the Church and the state led to different practical solutions. In many countries, hostile separation was the norm. This supposed that the state has an ideological option, which differs from the religions, and so separation also meant exclusion. The most obvious examples to this were the Communist countries, where the atheist ideology of Marxism-Leninism filled the role of more or less a state religion, but they also spoke about the separation of Church and state. However, secularism can also be an ideology, which results in the negative examples of separation.

But almost everywhere, even where the separation is cooperative and peaceful, the legislator requires that Churches and religious communities obey the laws. This supposes that society has a broader ideological horizon on which laws are established. But by giving up the principle of the natural law and by a weakening of the belief in the rationality of the world, the question arose: what is the basis of the law? If it is merely the decision of the so-called democratic majority formed in a given way, then the phenomenon, of which so many complain these days, is quite understandable: that is the weakening of trust in the law. Even the majority can end up with wrong or harmful decisions, especially if the concept of the common good becomes uncertain because there is no consensus even on the anthropological foundations of law. That is why it is difficult for the state to decide what is good for man. But the greater part of the society of the Western world lives in the hope that "in the event of a conflict there is an independent judge, who passes a just verdict on a fair legal basis." Their starting point is that "a legal system—no matter how debatable its rationality is in certain cases—on the whole still brings harmony both to the common good and people's individual interests."[26] This also highlights the problems of these unstable presumptions; namely, the uncertainty surrounding the concept of the common good and doubts about fair treatment on the part of the authorities.

Another basic change that we are witnessing is a shaking of the anthropological foundations of democracy. Western democracies presume that politicians and parties present and defend their political programs on a rational basis and that mature and responsible citizens make their choices and elect people using rational arguments. Today, this sounds like a utopia. First of all because the picture of reality has become very complicated thanks to the development of the sciences. In other words, there has to be a lot of trust for someone to believe the basic premises of a political program so that the elected body, based on a democratic majority, can count on the trust of that society. It seems to be a vicious circle. We have to place our trust in somebody in anticipation in order to let such a decision pass, in which we can trust.

From this point of view, the statement of Pope Francis in the autumn of 2014 in Strasbourg, speaking to the Council

---

[26] Udo Di Fabio, *Rechsordnung und Vertrauen*, in: *Neues Vertrauen in Staat, Kirche und Gesellschaft, Essener Gespäche zum Thema Staat und Kirche 50*, Münster: Aschendorff, 2017, pp. 61-68:62.

of Europe, seems to be significant. Here he expressed his concerns about the new interpretation of human rights: "I think particularly of the role of the European Court of Human Rights, which in some way represents the conscience of Europe with regard to those rights. I express my hope that this conscience will continue to mature, not through a simple consensus between parties, but as the result of efforts to build on those deep roots which are the bases on which the founders of contemporary Europe determined to build."[27]

So, fundamental rights, or the so-called human rights, should be based on an existing reality and on a certain morality, not simply on a majority decision of a body. That is, they have to have a content basis too, not just a formal basis.

But the new forms of communication make it possible that on the web and especially on the social media we acquire, a great amount of audiovisual impressions. And we react to those, maybe simply with a smiley, without discerning or drawing any conclusions.

New Technologies for Regulating Social Behavior Without Law and Morals

Information Technological, Genetic, and Other Biological (Psychological) Manipulations

A tendency can be clearly seen, which may not be a conscious aim, an intentional pursuit, but it derives from the

---

[27]   http://w2.vatican.va/content/francesco/en/speeches/2014/november/documents/papa-francesco_20141125_strasburgo-consiglio-europa.html.

dynamics of the situation. There is the possibility, or even a need or necessity, that social behavior can be regulated on a psychological, biological, genetic and, of course, economic basis. Here, law and morals may seem to be unnecessary. But these control mechanisms do have a serious disadvantage. They influence human activity by avoiding deliberate human decisions, and so they leave only a small place for human freedom and dignity. It is also a question whether, really, they can function independently without the state and without the law, because now all these systems expect the state and the law to guarantee that they work properly.

Super-Human Ambitions, and the Danger of Splitting Humanity into Two. The Uncertainty of the Concept of the Human Person, Individual Life and Death

Among the results of the natural sciences, the possibility of genetic engineering, creating super-humans, also arose.[28] And this—according to many experts—increases the danger of splitting humankind into two categories: natural-humans and super-humans. Another possibility is saving the contents of our brains on an external data-storage, maybe even without the permission of the person involved. Still, it remains a question whether the rationally perceivable contents behave differently within a given living body than outside it. Also, the issue of artificial intelligence is a real, present-day possibility, not a remote theory. The perspective of joining the artificial intelligence and the living body

---

[28] Cf. Robin L. Smith - Max Gomez, *Cells are the New Cure. The Cutting Edge Medical Breakthroughs that are Transforming our Health*, Dallas TX: BenBella Books, 2017, pp. 188-222.

is also a relevant question. Someone said poetically that Mephistopheles uploads Faust's brain to the cloud and downloads the artificial intelligence into a being.

All these questions show us that the question *what is man?* has deepened, and it seems as if the concepts of individual life and death have become uncertain or even detached. All this would remain in the world of science-fiction if the development of the natural sciences did not bring these matters so close to everyday life.

Problems

In all these areas, as well as others, scientific and techno-logical research produces new results so quickly that neither the legal regulations of the given areas nor moral reflec-tion can keep up with it. Basically, for both legal and moral evaluations, one needs to describe actual facts so that others can make their legal and moral deductions. But the discov-eries open new levels of reality, so the description of facts needed for moral evaluation and legal treatment are falling behind. In certain cases, this might be valid for complex economic processes too, where the public can feel as if the law and morals fall far behind real situations.

In light of the discoveries of the natural sciences, we can see again and again that human concepts and categories are too narrow to assimilate this new data, and the limits of the human brain are revealed. This is not surprising since the universe was not created by humans.

It seems that the secular state and the different world-views offering their reflections—especially religions—share the same fate. They both have to face such a new challenge that surpasses their habitual ways of functioning. But at the same time, the signs of distrust are also present. On the one hand, there is the lack of clear ideological foundations in the public thinking, because of which the distrust against the law and state gets more and more widespread. On the other hand—because of religious and cultural plurality—the states themselves look at the religious communities with suspicion, especially those who have only been present for a short time in their country, because they think that not all religious communities are able to or intend to accept the expected behavioral minimum of the secular state. Also, the modern state often looks suspiciously at the need of faith and religions for absolute truth. This is a question which was never answered definitively and satisfactorily in a secular state.[29] It seems that in the depths of a clearly secular state and legal system there is a tacit ideology, the content and foundations of which are less and less clear.

One alternative could see the state establishing a special relationship with the culturally important religion or religions, which considers the heritage of the values within a society but also guarantees religious freedom for everybody. It is here, where the statements of *Dignitatis humanae*, the declaration of the Second Vatican Council, appear in a new light. According to these, the basis of religious freedom is not that there is no truth in the matter of faith and religion, but on the contrary, the recognition of the fact that there is such a truth and man should seek it, but that human dignity requires it to be free of any exterior coercion.[30]

---

[29]   Cf. Di Fabio *Rechtsordnung* p. 63.
[30]   *Dignitatis humanae* 2-3.

CONCLUSIONS

Religion, and Especially the Judeo–Christian Heritage, Makes Possible a Personal Relationship With the Absolute

Religion, and especially the Judeo-Christian religion, is not simply a collection of moral rules, but so much more than this. It allows a personal relationship with the Absolute, the Almighty, who appears as a Creator in the context of the universe, whose wisdom and word (*logos*) penetrates the whole world. This means that our relationship with reality does not require an arbitrary pursuit in a meaningless or unknowable medium, but it fits into the context of an ultimate wisdom and love.

Some of the ideas at the core of the Christian tradition, such as the necessity of investigating the contingent world and the inherent intelligibility of the physical world, present a strong argument for a religious historical core of all sciences. Science seems to point beyond itself to some sort of Creative ground and reason for the contingent but rational order of the universe.[31]

The expressions of the requirements of morals can be very diverse. On the one hand, we are able to describe facts with the help of our concepts and to classify them, and to construct moral rules. If you like, we can look for the answer of Halakha to the situations of life. But similarly, we are sensitive to models of upright human behavior in a story, picture, or description without forming abstract laws. We can say that we let ourselves to be touched and carried

---

[31] See e.g. Ian Barbour, *Religion and Sciene: Historical and Contemporary Issue*, London: SCM, 1998, p. 91.

away by the enchantment of the Haggadah. Jesus, too, could express himself in commands or use parables, and what is more, he also passed onto his disciples the powerful example of his unforgettable deeds. We are heirs of such moral guidance, which is much more than just concepts and definitions.

We Have to Strive for Religious and Moral Reflection on the New Situations and Scientific Discoveries, Even If It Happens With a Delay

Even though the rapid progress of the natural sciences always provides us with new situations, we cannot grow weary of proclaiming basic moral values, and we have to apply moral reflection on these new situations, even if it is always late or does not turn out to be conceptual or verbal.

The Contribution of Religion to the Life of Society

Regarding all these challenges, many feel that we have to strive for so-called sustainable development not only in the field of economic life and not only to avoid the destruction of our environment. It is possible also in the field of science that, without legal or moral boundaries, the result would work for the destruction of mankind instead of for its happiness. Naturally, the basis of this notion is also the feeling or the belief that it is better if mankind exists than if not. So, the need for sustainable development arises in the field of the sciences too. But which explorer, which research center, which country would say that they should slow down in producing results or simply not research certain important areas? Everyone is convinced that in this case, the others would overtake them, and they fall behind in the race. What can we do? Even the ecological footprint of mankind is bigger than is sustainable in the long run. Shall we desperately join Hamlet and say together: "the time is out of joint"?

And this is where somebody can feel, based on many religious traditions, that they need some kind of salvation, that our own strength is not enough to solve our problems.

I am a Christian theologian, and to me the Providence of the Christian faith can bear some resemblance to theological proposals made in other religious traditions, such as the thought of the "great river" in other religions, but it is more personal than that. Already in the book of Genesis, we can read that "God saw all he had made, and indeed it was very good."[32] The Judeo-Christian heritage contains the belief that behind the whole universe there is a personal and benevolent Creator who revealed himself and wants to communicate with man.[33] And this, beyond giving a basic

---

[32]   Gn 1:31.

[33]   According to our Christian faith, the centre of the communication with God is Jesus Christ, whom we confess as our Lord and Master. He is the objective basis of our faith and therefore research into the historical Jesus or the historical Christ is the central question of today's Christian Theology. See e.g., Joseph Ratzinger (Pope Benedict XVI), *Jesus of Nazareth*, 3 vols., Ignatius Press, 2013; John P. Meier, *A Marginal Jew. Rethinking the Historical Jesus*, 5 vols., New York: Random House – Yale University Press, 1991-2016; *Handbook for the Study of the Historical Jesus*, ed. Tom Holmén – Stanley E. Porter, 4 vols., Leiden-Boston: Brill, 2011; cf. Nicola Ciola – Antonio Pitta – Giuseppe Pulcinelli, *Ricerca storica su Gesù. Bilanci e prospettive*, Bologna: EDB, 2017.

moral point of view, gives something extra, which is even more important. It generates trust both in the individual and in the community. It generates trust that even though our cognitive abilities cannot keep up with the fullness of reality, we can always somehow reach the necessary knowledge and cognitions. So, the weakness of our recognition is not a reason to give up our pursuit of the truth, and our striving for upright behavior.

Thank you for your attention!